OMG WTF DOES THE CONSTITUTION ACTUALLY SAY?

OMG WTF DOES THE CONSTITUTION ACTUALLY SAY?

A NON-BORING GUIDE TO HOW OUR DEMOCRACY IS SUPPOSED TO WORK

BEN SHEEHAN

BLACK DOG
& LEVENTHAL
PUBLISHERS
NEW YORK

Black Dog & Leventhal Publishers
Hachette Book Group
1290 Avenue of the Americas
New York, NY 10104

www.hachettebookgroup.com
www.blackdogandleventhal.com

First Edition: April 2020

Black Dog & Leventhal Publishers is an imprint of Perseus Books, LLC, a subsidiary of Hachette Book Group, Inc. The Black Dog & Leventhal Publishers name and logo are trademarks of Hachette Book Group, Inc.

Front cover images courtesy of Library of Congress (James Madison) and Getty Images (Constitution pages)

Interior images courtesy Shutterstock: vii, 3, 7, 20, 23, 27, 31, 32, 45, 46, 55, 64, 67, 71, 73, 75, 79, 80, 87, 89, 97, 111, 146, 155, 161, 175, 192; and Getty Images: 1, 15, 30, 51, 59, 61, 141, 148, 175

Constitution and Declaration of Independence text courtesy of the National Archives.

The publisher is not responsible for websites (or their content) that are not owned by the publisher.

The Hachette Speakers Bureau provides a wide range of authors for speaking events.
To find out more, go to www.HachetteSpeakersBureau.com or call (866) 376-6591.

Print book interior design by Chad W. Beckerman

LCCN: 2019950074
ISBNs: 978-0-7624-9848-2 (paper over board),
978-0-7624-9846-8 (ebook)

Printed in the United States of America

LSC-C

1 2 3 4 5 6 7 8 9 10

For my mom,
who taught me this stuff over dinner.

For my dad,
who taught me how to simplify.

CONTENTS

PRE-PREAMBLE

The Constitution is America's instruction manual. Think of it as our "Terms and Conditions," because like other terms and conditions most of us don't know what the fuck is in it. Only 39 percent of American adults can name the 3 branches of government despite their being outlined in the Constitution's first 3 articles. It's weird that a country run by "the People" is full of people who don't know how it runs. I'm not a conspiracy theorist, but it seems convenient—for some—that most of us are in the dark. If we don't know how our government works, it's hard for us to hold our elected leaders accountable. In a way, our ignorance is their permanence and also JUST KIDDING, I AM A CONSPIRACY THEORIST. IT'S A CONSPIRACY.

Looking at our education system today, I don't really get why most schools shoehorn "how government works" into U.S. history or social studies. It feels like a class that deserves exclusive focus. Growing up I remember nodding along to the names of our founders, the dates of pivotal events, and the stories of how we came to be. They're all interesting to an extent, but I also felt like we were BOMBARDED BY HISTORY. Teachers were SO PUMPED about America's beginnings that the actual info on how it functions was lost. Often times I just wanted someone to say, "Here's how our government works, and here's how you can affect it."

BTW

Having said that—when I feel like context *is* needed—I'll throw it here. "BTW" gives background, "FYI" defines stuff, "IMO" proposes things, and "N/A" means it no longer applies. Read them, skip them, or alternate. Do *you*.

United States Terms and Conditions

I have read and agree to the United States Terms & Conditions

Cancel   Accept

FYI

It's good to know terms. The "federal" government applies to all states and territories, which each has their own government. In addition to the 50 states there are 5 permanently inhabited territories—American Samoa (51,000 people), the Northern Mariana Islands (52,000 people), the U.S. Virgin Islands (107,000 people), Guam (167,000 people), and Puerto Rico (3.3 million people). American Samoa, the Northern Mariana Islands, and Puerto Rico have their own constitutions—as does each state—and the Northern Mariana Islands and Puerto Rico are "commonwealths" where Congress can't take away their right to self-government (in this meaning of the word). But unlike states, territories lack congressional voting representation and the ability to vote for president (and for American Samoa, U.S. citizenship). There are also 9 permanently uninhabited territories—Baker Island, Howland Island, Jarvis Island, Johnston Atoll, Kingman Reef, Midway Atoll (40 wildlife workers), Navassa Island, Palmyra Atoll (20 scientists), and Wake Island (100 military personnel), and 2 *disputed* uninhabited territories— Bajo Nuevo Bank (disputed with Colombia) and Serranilla Bank (disputed with Colombia and Honduras). The federal government also governs Washington, D.C. (720,000 people), aka the seat of government, and it affects U.S. citizens living abroad. But the 573 federally recognized Native American tribes, on 326 federally administered reservations, with 1.2 million residents total, are largely left to local control. And then within states and territories there are cities, counties, towns, townships, and school districts with their own local governments. But this book covers the federal government and parts of state governments, since that's what our Constitution establishes. Now that you know the federal government's entire jurisdiction, let's continue.

Because, in truth, I find our historical fixation sort of masturbatory, to the point of muddying the actual rules. It's like approaching a recipe by analyzing the mind-set of the chef when he devised it. Were there exigent circumstances at the time of his cooking? Were his ingredients limited because of weather conditions or a lack of proximity to trade? Did he consider other chefs' approaches before attempting his own? This may bring greater understanding to the dish, but also, just tell me how to make the fucking quiche.

50 STATES

Alabama Alaska Arizona Arkansas California Colorado Connecticut

Delaware Florida Georgia Hawaii Idaho Illinois Indiana

Iowa Kansas Kentucky Louisiana Maine Maryland Massachusetts

Michigan Minnesota Mississippi Missouri

Montana Nebraska Nevada New Hampshire

Washington D.C.

New Jersey New Mexico New York North Carolina North Dakota Ohio Oklahoma

Oregon Pennsylvania Rhode Island South Carolina South Dakota Tennessee Texas

Utah Vermont Virginia Washington West Virginia Wisconsin Wyoming

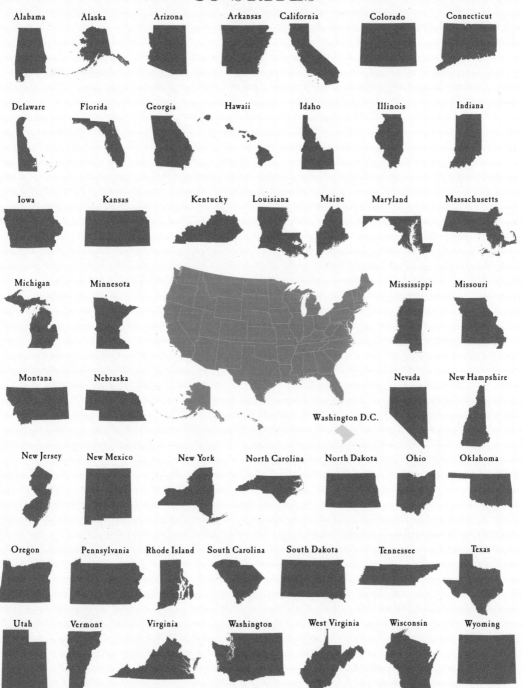

PERMANENTLY INHABITED TERRITORIES

American Samoa Guam Northern Mariana Islands Puerto Rico U.S. Virgin Islands

I guess what I'm describing is the difference between U.S. history and civics. U.S. history leans on memorization and passive learning, while civics is our participation toolkit, the study of government and the rights and responsibilities of being a citizen. These include understanding how government works, at all levels, and knowing how we can use it to better our lives. But right now, our schools teach WAY more U.S. history than civics. As of this writing, 30 states require at least a year of U.S. history, while only 8 states require a year of civics *or* government. If we only spent a year learning how to read between kindergarten and 12th grade, we'd also suck at it. Maybe that's why proficiency in civics across K–12 hasn't reached 30 percent in the last decade. But civics isn't some ditchable elective—it's vital stuff. George Washington even tried to create a national university around it. In his 8th (and final) State of the Union address, he told Congress,

> a primary object of such a national institution should be the education of our youth in the science of Government. In a Republic, what species of knowledge can be equally important? and what duty more pressing on its Legislature, than to patronize a plan for communicating it to those who are to be the future guardians of the liberties of the country?

So, our first president thought it was the most important subject, and 224 years later just 8 states require a year of it. Great job, everyone!!

The idea for this book came about last year; I was cleaning my apartment when I came across my pocket Constitution from 8th grade (I was lucky my school distributed them). Out of curiosity, I decided to reread it. And honestly? It was *rough*. I know it's 200+ years old, but the punctuation seemed picked from a hat. The sentences are *dense*. The phrasing is odd. For something so important it struck me how inaccessible it was. We can argue about grammar and whether it's a necessity or a classist relic, but let's be honest: If someone wrote and spoke in the style of the Constitution today, you would keep postponing plans with them.

In September of 1789—6 months after the Constitution took effect—Thomas Jefferson wrote to James Madison about treating constitutions as living works, so that past generations didn't force outdated principles onto future ones.

> Every constitution then, and every law, naturally expires at the end of 19 years. If it be enforced longer, it is an act of force, and not of right.

I don't know about brand-new constitutions every 19 years, but I do know that—of every country in the world—we have the oldest constitution still in use. So at a minimum, I can support updating its presentation every few years so that new generations can grasp it. Because before we decide to change the Constitution—or fight to keep it—we should know what it actually says. And while it's true that the Constitution was originally written by a few of us, just for *some* of us, today it belongs to all of us. We have a right to know what's inside.

And lastly, I wanted to make sure that, in the process of paraphrasing the Constitution, I wasn't just injecting my bias. So I tried to note my opinions, while also running this book by multiple constitutional experts for their thoughts and feedback.

BTW

Yes, there are conflicting constitutional interpretations; ⅓ of the federal government (the judicial branch) is devoted to it. But while some of the Constitution has caused centuries of debate, I believe most of its information is straightforward, if oddly styled.

I've also included the Constitution's original text, for reference, and I've added the Declaration of Independence. It isn't part of the Constitution, but it did set the table for it.

So without further ado, here is a non-boring guide to the U.S. Constitution.

ARTICLES OF THE CONSTITUTION

Preamble

We the People of the United States, in Order to form a more perfect Union, establish Justice, insure domestic Tranquility, provide for the common defence, promote the general Welfare, and secure the Blessings of Liberty to ourselves and our Posterity, do ordain and establish this Constitution for the United States of America.

PREAMBLE

Some Europeans are starting a country that will provide justice, peace, safety, and freedom. It will ensure fairness, stop uprisings and invasions, and protect people's rights. The country will also facilitate the health, happiness, and prosperity of its people. The people will run this country.

BTW

55 guys of European descent—or "delegates" from 12 of the 13 states (minus Rhode Island)—attended the Constitutional Convention in Philadelphia from May 25 to September 17, 1787. The number of delegates eventually dwindled from 55 to 41, and 39 ended up signing the Constitution—32 English, Irish, Scottish, Welsh, or Dutch descendants and 7 English, Irish, or Scottish immigrants. But as for "liberty," half of the delegates owned slaves. Slaves were almost 20 percent of the population in 1787, so the justice, peace, safety, freedom, health, happiness, and prosperity parts didn't apply to everyone...but the amendments would eventually help.

Signed (Y/N)
Delegates without a letter weren't present on signing day

CONNECTICUT
Oliver Elsworth
William Samuel Johnson (Y)
Roger Sherman (Y)

DELAWARE
Richard Bassett (Y)
Gunning Bedford, Jr. (Y)
Jacob Broom (Y)
John Dickinson (Y—Was sick, wasn't there)
George Read (Y—Also signed for his friend John)

GEORGIA
Abraham Baldwin (Y)
William Few (Y)
William Houston
William L. Pierce

MARYLAND
Daniel Carroll (Y)
Daniel of St. Thomas Jenifer (Y)
Luther Martin
James McHenry (Y)
John F. Mercer

MASSACHUSETTS
Elbridge Gerry (N)
Nathaniel Gorham (Y)
Rufus King (Y)
Caleb Strong

NEW HAMPSHIRE
Nicholas Gilman (Y)
John Langdon (Y)

NEW JERSEY
David Brearley (Y)
Jonathan Dayton (Y)
William C. Houston
William Livingston (Y)
William Paterson (Y)

NEW YORK
Alexander Hamilton (Y)
John Lansing, Jr.
Robert Yates

NORTH CAROLINA
William Blount (Y)
William R. Davie
Alexander Martin
Richard. Dobbs Spaight (Y)
Hugh Williamson (Y)

PENNSYLVANIA
George Clymer (Y)
Thomas Fitzsimons (Y)
Benjamin Franklin (Y)
Jared Ingersoll (Y)
Thomas Mifflin (Y)
Gouverneur Morris (Y)
Robert Morris (Y)
James Wilson (Y)

RHODE ISLAND
No one came.

SOUTH CAROLINA
Pierce Butler (Y)
Charles Pinckney (Y)
Charles Cotesworth Pinckney (Y)
John Rutledge (Y)

VIRGINIA
John Blair (Y)
James Madison Jr. (Y)
George Mason (N)
James McClurg
Edmund J. Randolph (N)
George Washington (Y—Also Convention President)
George Wythe

ARTICLE I: Section 1

All legislative Powers herein granted shall be vested in a Congress of the United States, which shall consist of a Senate and House of Representatives.

CONGRESS (AKA THE LEGISLATIVE BRANCH)
10 SECTIONS
ARTICLE I: SECTION 1

An Overview

FYI

Our government is a "republic" because we send people to Congress to make our decisions for us (it would be hard for the whole population to make every decision). But it's also a "democracy" because those people, or "representatives," are democratically elected by us. Therefore, America is a representative democracy or a democratic republic (fun terms that roll off the tongue).

"Congress," our federal legislature, is the House of Representatives *and* the Senate. Congress, and ONLY Congress, writes our laws—but only the ones the Constitution says it can.

FYI

Many people believe Congress *only* means the House of Representatives. While "Congress" and "the House" are sometimes used interchangeably, THIS IS WRONG. Also, because Congress has *2 chambers*—the House *and* the Senate—it's "bicameral" and not "unicameral." You now know more about Congress than a shitload of people (and potentially some members of Congress).

ARTICLE I: Section 2

The House of Representatives shall be composed of Members chosen every second Year by the People of the several States, and the Electors in each State shall have the Qualifications requisite for Electors of the most numerous Branch of the State Legislature.

No Person shall be a Representative who shall not have attained to the Age of twenty five Years, and been seven Years a Citizen of the United States, and who shall not, when elected, be an Inhabitant of that State in which he shall be chosen.

Representatives and direct Taxes shall be apportioned among the several States which may be included within this Union, according to their respective Numbers, which shall be determined by adding to the whole Number of free Persons, including those bound to Service for a Term of Years, and excluding Indians not taxed, three fifths of all other Persons. The actual Enumeration shall be made within three Years after the first Meeting of the Congress of the United States, and within every subsequent Term of ten Years, in such Manner as they shall by Law direct. The Number of Representatives shall not exceed one for every thirty Thousand, but each State shall have at Least one Representative; and until such enumeration shall be made, the State of New Hampshire shall be entitled to chuse three, Massachusetts eight, Rhode-Island and Providence Plantations one, Connecticut five, New-York six, New Jersey four, Pennsylvania eight, Delaware one, Maryland six, Virginia ten, North Carolina five, South Carolina five, and Georgia three.

When vacancies happen in the Representation from any State, the Executive Authority thereof shall issue Writs of Election to fill such Vacancies.

The House of Representatives shall chuse their Speaker and other Officers; and shall have the sole Power of Impeachment.

ARTICLE I: SECTION 2
The House

Every 2 years the whole House is up for re-election. If you can vote in your *state's* house elections, you can vote in your state's *U.S. House* elections.

FYI

This is a good time to note that other than Nebraska (which has a "unicameral" legislature), each state has its *own* house and senate for writing state laws. Sometimes a state house is called a house of delegates, or a state assembly, or *also* a house of representatives (confusing), while a state senate is sometimes called a senate (also confusing). Point is—besides Nebraska—each state has a house and a senate that are separate from the U.S. House and the U.S. Senate (which write *federal* laws). Please do not be ashamed if you didn't know this. Also, to make it easier, the capitalized "House" and "Senate" will mean the federal legislature and the lowercase "house" and "senate" will mean a state legislature.

The residents of each state elect its representatives to the House, and the number of representatives is proportional to each state's population (i.e., bigger states get more representatives). The only requirements to be a U.S. representative are:

★ You must be at least 25 years old.
★ You must have been an American citizen for at least 7 years.
★ You must live in the state you're representing.
★ Nothing else.

N/A

The next part of Article I, Section 2 no longer applies. Also, it was fucked up! It said that when counting the U.S. population for the purposes of establishing federal taxes (we used to tax states based on their population, where states paid taxes "per head") and determining each state's number of U.S. representatives in the House, "free people" counted as 1. People "working" for a *fixed* amount of time (i.e., indentured servants) counted as 1 as well. Native Americans who didn't pay taxes counted as 0. And everyone else (i.e., slaves) counted as ⅗—or 60 percent—of a person. The idea was that if slaves counted as whole people, the slaveholding states would have to pay more in federal tax. But slaves counting as people would also give slaveholding states more representatives in the House. So James Wilson and Charles Pinckney (2 of the delegates) suggested the ⅗ compromise, an unused idea that James Madison had come up with for the old constitution (aka the Articles of Confederation). Anyway, this fucked-up part of the Constitution was eliminated by the 13th and 14th Amendments.

The number of U.S. representatives from each state must be determined within 3 years of the first meeting of Congress (the first determination was in 1790) and revised every 10 years after that. Congress decides how this is done.

FYI

This is called the Census. We count the population, and the federal government uses the data to decide how many representatives each state gets (this isn't in the Constitution, but the government also uses it to determine how much federal funding goes to things like roads, healthcare, and disaster relief). Regardless of population, each state gets at least 1 representative (states with only 1 are called "at large").

N/A

You can ignore the next part of the Constitution—it was just a list of existing states and the number of representatives they got in the 1st Congress (in 1789). At the time, states got 1 representative for every 30,000 people, but as the population grew—and more representatives were added—the House got crowded. So, 140 years later, Congress passed the Reapportionment Act of 1929 that capped the number of U.S. representatives at 435 (which we still have today). But since we're locked at 435, and have been for 91 years, there is now 1 U.S. representative for every 752,000 people instead of every 30,000—or 25 times more than the delegates intended.

> **Each state must have at least 1 representative. When a representative leaves office before the end of their term (quits, dies, gets kicked out), the governor of that representative's state calls for a special election to fill the seat.**
>
> **Representatives choose their leader—the speaker of the House—and other officers (visit bit.ly/headsofhouse for the list; don't worry, it's just a shortened link to the House's website).**

BTW

There is absolutely no rule for who can be the speaker, meaning the Constitution has no requirements for it. The speaker of the House could be you, your dad, your dad's friend, your sister, Blake Shelton, anyone. So far it has never NOT been a current member of the House, but nowhere in the Constitution does it say that it needs to be. If Blake Shelton gets a majority of votes from the representatives and agrees to do it, Blake Shelton becomes speaker of the House. He would also be 2nd in line for the presidency, behind the vice president. Good luck, Blake!

Finally, just the House—NOT the Senate, the president, the courts, or anyone or anything else—has the power to impeach.

FYI

"Impeach" DOES NOT MEAN "remove from office"; it only means the Senate can begin DECIDING, with a trial, whether or not to remove someone (including the president, other executive branch officers, judges, and Supreme Court justices). We'll dive into impeachment later, but think of it as the House charging a federal official with a crime, and the Senate as the courtroom trial where the punishment is removal.

Speaking of...

ARTICLE I: Section 3

The Senate of the United States shall be composed of two Senators from each State, chosen by the Legislature thereof, for six Years; and each Senator shall have one Vote.

Immediately after they shall be assembled in Consequence of the first Election, they shall be divided as equally as may be into three Classes. The Seats of the Senators of the first Class shall be vacated at the Expiration of the second Year, of the second Class at the Expiration of the fourth Year, and of the third Class at the Expiration of the sixth Year, so that one third may be chosen every second Year; and if Vacancies happen by Resignation, or otherwise, during the Recess of the Legislature of any State, the Executive thereof may make temporary Appointments until the next Meeting of the Legislature, which shall then fill such Vacancies.

No Person shall be a Senator who shall not have attained to the Age of thirty Years, and been nine Years a Citizen of the United States, and who shall not, when elected, be an

Inhabitant of that State for which he shall be chosen.

The Vice President of the United States shall be President of the Senate, but shall have no Vote, unless they be equally divided.

The Senate shall chuse their other Officers, and also a President pro tempore, in the Absence of the Vice President, or when he shall exercise the Office of President of the United States.

The Senate shall have the sole Power to try all Impeachments. When sitting for that Purpose, they shall be on Oath or Affirmation. When the President of the United States is tried, the Chief Justice shall preside: And no Person shall be convicted without the Concurrence of two thirds of the Members present.

Judgment in Cases of Impeachment shall not extend further than to removal from Office, and disqualification to hold and enjoy any Office of honor, Trust or Profit under the United States: but the Party convicted shall nevertheless be liable and subject to Indictment, Trial, Judgment and Punishment, according to Law.

ARTICLE I: SECTION 3

The Senate

Every state has 2 U.S. senators who serve 6-year terms. Senators have 1 vote in the Senate, and the votes carry equal weight.

N/A

It is no longer relevant, but we didn't always pick U.S. senators. Until 1913, state legislatures—state houses and state senates—chose them. If a state legislature wasn't in session when a U.S. Senate seat became vacant (if a senator quit or died), the governor of that senator's state would appoint a temporary senator until the legislature could choose a replacement. Thanks to the 17th Amendment, citizens now pick their U.S. senators like they pick U.S. representatives—by directly voting for them after months of incessant fundraising emails, text messages, and Facebook ads.

The Senate is divided into thirds. Every 2 years, ⅓ of the Senate is up for re-election.

FYI

There weren't 50 states (i.e., 100 senators) when the Constitution was written, so it wasn't the plan to have a long-term number not divisible by 3. But after the first congressional election, senators were divided into 3 "classes"—Class 1, Class 2, Class 3—and as new states formed, their senators were added to these classes to keep them relatively even.

The only requirements to be a U.S. senator are:

* ★ You must be at least 30 years old.
* ★ You must have been an American citizen for at least 9 years.
* ★ You must live in the state you're representing.
* ★ That's it.

Oddly, the vice president is *also* the Senate president, but they can only vote to break a tie. When the VP is unavailable, the Senate president "pro tempore" ("for a time" in Latin) runs the Senate. Senators pick this "president pro tempore" and other officers (visit bit.ly/headsofsenate for a list; again, this is just a link to the Senate's website).

BTW

Like "speaker of the House," the Constitution doesn't specify any eligibility requirements for the president pro tempore. It does NOT say it needs to be a senator. Usually it is the most senior senator in the majority party, but this is customary. If Lionel Richie gets a majority of Senate votes and agrees to do it, Lionel Richie becomes the Senate president pro tempore, and 3rd in line for the presidency. Also, with *The Voice* running the House, we need checks and balances.

As you may remember, *only the Senate* tries impeachments. During an impeachment trial the senators are under oath or affirmation ("affirmation" is an oath without the religious context). If the president is being tried, the chief justice of the Supreme Court presides. Two-thirds of senators (67) are needed to convict, and the punishment can't go beyond removal from office and an inability to hold future federal office. Finally, the person convicted can still be tried for crimes *after* being removed. So try not to get impeached and removed—changing careers is hard enough without the threat of jail.

BTW

Andrew Johnson, Bill Clinton, and Donald Trump are the only presidents to have been impeached. People think Richard Nixon was impeached, but he actually resigned before the House could vote. And neither Johnson nor Clinton (nor, as of this writing, Trump) was removed from office. But ever since Nixon's investigation, there has been ongoing debate over whether a sitting federal official can be charged with a crime and tried *without* being impeached and removed. In 1973 and 2000, a Justice Department memo said "no." In 1974 and 1998, a memo to the Independent Counsel (the presidential investigator) said "yes." The issue isn't in the Constitution, so it's unclear. Anyway, there's more impeachment stuff in Article II, so get pumped.

ARTICLE I: Section 4

The Times, Places and Manner of holding Elections for Senators and Representatives, shall be prescribed in each State by the Legislature thereof; but the Congress may at any time by Law make or alter such Regulations, except as to the Places of chusing Senators.

 The Congress shall assemble at least once in every Year, and such Meeting shall be on the first Monday in December, unless they shall by Law appoint a different Day.

ARTICLE I: SECTION 4
Congressional Elections and Meetings

State legislatures decide when, where, and how to hold elections for U.S. representatives and senators.

IMO

In 1842, Congress mandated that "districts" be used to elect U.S. representatives and to decide which representative represents which people in a state. Districts are sometimes drawn by the state's legislature, or by an independent commission, or by a committee of politicians and/or political appointees. The process is called "redistricting."

However, if a state legislature or political committee draws the districts—and is dominated by one party—it can manipulate these districts to *help* the party. This process is called "partisan gerrymandering," and it's done by "packing" the other party's voters into a few districts (so there are fewer of those voters in other districts) or by "cracking" the other party's voters across many districts (so those voters will always be in the minority). Partisan gerrymandering allows state legislatures and political committees to fix the outcomes of House and state legislative elections BEFORE THEY HAPPEN.

As for why this is legal, the Supreme Court has found constitutional grounds to ban gerrymandering based on voters' race but NOT their political party. I personally think Congress should pass a law, or propose an amendment, to ban partisan gerrymandering. Until that happens, each state should give redistricting responsibilities to independent commissions—not to state legislatures or politician committees—so that the process isn't corrupted by partisanship.

Depending on the state, the legislature can pass a law, or voters can pass a ballot measure, or the state can amend its constitution. Anyway, both parties still do this shit—choosing their voters instead of the opposite—and it's a huge rot in our democracy. Dark stuff!

But Congress can pass a law to override the state legislatures on this, *except* for the part about where Senate elections are held (this is a holdover from when state legislatures elected senators).

IMO

In 1845, Congress passed a law establishing Election Day as the Tuesday after the 1st Monday in November. They set a uniform date so that one state's results didn't influence another's. However, the reason they chose *this* date was because there were so many farmers in 1845 that Congress didn't want to interfere with their planting and harvesting schedules. Today, Congress could change this 175-year-old law so that people don't have to skip work to vote, since many states allow limited windows to do so. I personally think Congress should move Election Day to a Saturday, or establish a federal holiday, or combine it with Veterans Day (since voting is one right our veterans fought to protect). But I find it odd that the most important part of our democracy is still so inconvenient. And since they no longer need to travel 48 hours to vote like they did in 1845, I don't even think the farmers would mind.

Congress must meet at least once a year (they meet more than that).

N/A

It isn't relevant anymore, but if Congress did meet once a year, it had to be the 1st Monday in December. But the 12th Amendment changed this to January 3 at 12 p.m. and gave Congress the ability to change it to whenever it wants. A boring detail, but it's in here.

ARTICLE I: Section 5

Each House shall be the Judge of the Elections, Returns and Qualifications of its own Members, and a Majority of each shall constitute a Quorum to do Business; but a smaller Number may adjourn from day to day, and may be authorized to compel the Attendance of absent Members, in such Manner, and under such Penalties as each House may provide.

Each House may determine the Rules of its Proceedings, punish its Members for disorderly Behaviour, and, with the Concurrence of two thirds, expel a Member.

Each House shall keep a Journal of its Proceedings, and from time to time publish the same, excepting such Parts as may in their Judgment require Secrecy; and the Yeas and Nays of the Members of either House on any question shall, at the Desire of one fifth of those Present, be entered on the Journal.

Neither House, during the Session of Congress, shall, without the Consent of the other, adjourn for more than three days, nor to any other Place than that in which the two Houses shall be sitting.

ARTICLE I: SECTION 5
Congressional Rules and Proceedings

The House and the Senate judge their own elections and results, and it's their responsibility to vet the qualifications of their members (i.e., age, citizenship, residency). To do business, a "quorum" (minimum number) must be present, which is a majority of members. Day-to-day a smaller number can meet, collaborate, or hang out, and members can even require other members to show up, and punish them if they don't. The House and the Senate can also punish members for bad behavior, and they can expel a member with a ⅔ vote.

The House and the Senate must each keep a journal of activity, and publish it on occasion, redacting the secretive parts. The vote tallies ("Yeas" and "Nays") are entered into these journals if ⅕ of attending members say it's okay.

BTW

Journals aside, you can track how your representative and senators vote by visiting House.gov, Senate.gov, Congress.gov, GovInfo.gov (for the Congressional Record Index), or GovTrack.us, or be one of the 6 people watching live floor votes on C-SPAN.

Neither the House nor the Senate can break for more than 3 days while in session, or meet anywhere other than the Capitol, without the other's consent.

FYI

"Capitol" with an "o" is the building; "capital" with an "a" is the city (just in case).

ARTICLE I: Section 6

The Senators and Representatives shall receive a Compensation for their Services, to be ascertained by Law, and paid out of the Treasury of the United States. They shall in all Cases, except Treason, Felony and Breach of the Peace, be privileged from Arrest during their Attendance at the Session of their respective Houses, and in going to and returning from the same; and for any Speech or Debate in either House, they shall not be questioned in any other Place.

No Senator or Representative shall, during the Time for which he was elected, be appointed to any civil Office under the Authority of the United States, which shall have been created, or the Emoluments whereof shall have been encreased during such time; and no Person holding any Office under the United States, shall be a Member of either House during his Continuance in Office.

ARTICLE I: SECTION 6
Member Benefits and Rights

Representatives and senators earn salaries, and the amount is determined by law and paid from the U.S. treasury (aka our federal tax dollars).

Here are some rules for U.S. representatives and senators:

* They can't be arrested in, heading to, or coming from a session—except for treason, felony, or breach of peace (the last one is vague).
* They can't be questioned for anything mentioned during a speech or a debate in the Capitol.

BTW

This basically gives "freedom of speech" to members of Congress in a legislative context. For example, they can't be sued for defamation for something they say on the floor.

* They can't be appointed to an executive branch position, whether newly created or with a newly increased salary, before finishing their term.
* If you currently have an executive branch job, you can't become a U.S. representative or senator and still hold that job.

ARTICLE I: Section 7

All Bills for raising Revenue shall originate in the House of Representatives; but the Senate may propose or concur with Amendments as on other Bills.

Every Bill which shall have passed the House of Representatives and the Senate, shall, before it become a Law, be presented to the President of the United States; If he approve he shall sign it, but if not he shall return it, with his Objections to that House in which it shall have originated, who shall enter the Objections at large on their Journal, and proceed to reconsider it. If after such Reconsideration two thirds of that House shall agree to pass the Bill, it shall be sent, together with the Objections, to the other House, by which it shall likewise be reconsidered, and if approved by two thirds of that House, it shall become a Law. But in all such Cases the Votes of both Houses shall be determined by yeas and Nays, and the Names of the Persons voting for and against the Bill shall be entered on the Journal of each House respectively. If any Bill shall not be returned by the President within ten Days (Sundays excepted) after it shall have been presented to him, the Same shall be a Law, in like Manner as if he had signed it, unless the Congress by their Adjournment prevent its Return, in which Case it shall not be a Law.

Every Order, Resolution, or Vote to which the Concurrence of the Senate and House of Representatives may be necessary (except on a question of Adjournment) shall be presented to the President of the United States; and before the Same shall take Effect, shall be approved by him, or being disapproved by him, shall be repassed by two thirds of the Senate and House of Representatives, according to the Rules and Limitations prescribed in the Case of a Bill.

ARTICLE I: SECTION 7

How Bills Become Laws

Bills around taxes must start in the House. The Senate can agree with them or add to them like they do with other bills.

Now for the *Schoolhouse Rock* fan's favorite…

When a bill passes both the House and the Senate, it goes to the president (this is called "presentment"). The president can sign it, making it a law, or send it back with notes to the chamber where it started (this is called a "veto," but the term isn't in the Constitution). That chamber writes down the president's notes in their journal (I definitely didn't know journals were such a thing) and its members reevaluate the bill. If 2/3 of the House and the Senate approve the same version of the bill, regardless of the president's notes, it becomes a law (this is called a "veto override," but this term also isn't in the Constitution). The House and the Senate must write the yeas and nays of how members voted into their journals (again with the journals). If the president receives a bill from Congress but *doesn't* veto it within 10 days, not counting Sundays, it becomes a law. But if Congress *isn't* in session at the end of the 10 days, then the bill *doesn't* become a law (this is called a "pocket veto," but it's also not in here). Anyway, that's the *actual* process of how a bill becomes a law, so turn that into a fucking song.

FYI

It isn't in the Constitution, but Congress has its *own* process before a bill goes to the president. The House and the Senate both have committees and subcommittees with smaller numbers of members to handle specific issues (e.g., climate change, small businesses, foreign affairs). This is where most bills start. When a bill gets discussed in committee and the committee members vote to advance it, it goes to the larger committee (if it began in subcommittee) or to the whole House or Senate ("floor") for a vote. If it passes, it goes to the *other* chamber for a vote. If that chamber wants to add or remove things, instead of prolonging the

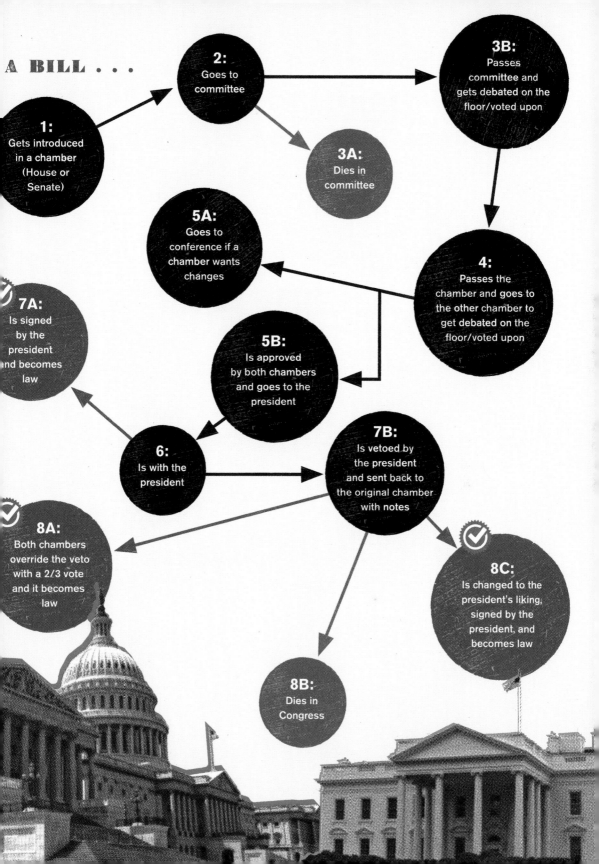

A BILL . . .

1: Gets introduced in a chamber (House or Senate)

2: Goes to committee

3A: Dies in committee

3B: Passes committee and gets debated on the floor/voted upon

4: Passes the chamber and goes to the other chamber to get debated on the floor/voted upon

5A: Goes to conference if a chamber wants changes

5B: Is approved by both chambers and goes to the president

6: Is with the president

7A: Is signed by the president and becomes law

7B: Is vetoed by the president and sent back to the original chamber with notes

8A: Both chambers override the veto with a 2/3 vote and it becomes law

8B: Dies in Congress

8C: Is changed to the president's liking, signed by the president, and becomes law

process by going back and forth between committees and chambers, the representatives and the senators meet "in conference" to hash out the details. The goal is to find one version of the bill to send to the president.

This process applies to all orders (bills), resolutions (same as bills), and votes where the House and the Senate must agree, *except* for ones about where and when Congress can adjourn.

BTW

According to the Declaration of Independence, King George III would make colony representatives gather at weird times—in weird places—to exhaust them into agreeing with him. So this is likely to protect against that.

ARTICLE I: Section 8

The Congress shall have Power To lay and collect Taxes, Duties, Imposts and Excises, to pay the Debts and provide for the common Defence and general Welfare of the United States; but all Duties, Imposts and Excises shall be uniform throughout the United States;

To borrow Money on the credit of the United States;

To regulate Commerce with foreign Nations, and among the several States, and with the Indian Tribes;

To establish an uniform Rule of Naturalization, and uniform Laws on the subject of Bankruptcies throughout the United States;

To coin Money, regulate the Value thereof, and of foreign Coin, and fix the Standard of Weights and Measures;

To provide for the Punishment of counterfeiting the Securities and current Coin of the United States;

To establish Post Offices and post Roads;

To promote the Progress of Science and useful Arts, by securing for limited Times to Authors and Inventors the exclusive Right to their respective Writings and Discoveries;

To constitute Tribunals inferior to the supreme Court;

To define and punish Piracies and Felonies committed on the high Seas, and Offences against the Law of Nations;

To declare War, grant Letters of Marque and Reprisal, and make Rules concerning Captures on Land and Water;

To raise and support Armies, but no Appropriation of Money to that Use shall be for a longer Term than two Years;

To provide and maintain a Navy;

To make Rules for the Government and Regulation of the land and naval Forces;

To provide for calling forth the Militia to execute the Laws of the Union, suppress Insurrections and repel Invasions;

To provide for organizing, arming, and disciplining, the Militia, and for governing such Part of them as may be employed in the Service of the United States, reserving to the States respectively, the Appointment of the Officers, and the Authority of training the Militia according to the discipline prescribed by Congress;

To exercise exclusive Legislation in all Cases whatsoever, over such District (not exceeding ten Miles square) as may, by Cession of particular States, and the Acceptance of Congress, become the Seat of the Government of the United States, and to exercise like Authority over all Places purchased by the Consent of the Legislature of the State in which the Same shall be, for the Erection of Forts, Magazines, Arsenals, dock-Yards, and other needful Buildings;—And

To make all Laws which shall be necessary and proper for carrying into Execution the foregoing Powers, and all other Powers vested by this Constitution in the Government of the United States, or in any Department or Officer thereof.

ARTICLE I: SECTION 8
Congressional Powers

Here are some things that Congress *can* do:

⋆ Set and collect taxes, duties, imposts, and excises for the purpose of paying down the national debt, financing national defense, and providing for the well-being of the country. Also these duties, imposts, and excises must be the same for everyone (but the taxes don't have to be).

FYI

"Duties" are taxes on imports and exports, "imposts" are taxes on imports, and "excises" are taxes on specific goods paid by the producer or merchant, not by the consumer directly (although they pay for it with a higher sales price). So the next time you're flying international, maybe take advantage of that Duty Free booze, cigarette, and cologne opportunity (but for God's sake, please don't wear the cologne on the plane).

⋆ Borrow money on U.S. credit.
⋆ Regulate commerce with other countries, between states, or with Native American tribes.
⋆ Lay out the process of becoming an American citizen.
⋆ Establish bankruptcy law.
⋆ Coin U.S. money and regulate its value.
⋆ Regulate the value of foreign money.
⋆ Set standard weights and measures (e.g., inches, feet, yards, miles, pounds, tons).
⋆ Punish the counterfeiting of money or securities (e.g., stocks, credit, bonds, options).
⋆ Establish post offices and post roads.

BTW

Post roads don't exist anymore, but these were roads JUST FOR MAIL. If you wanted to use them for traveling, you had to get government permission. It was like getting an HOV lane exemption for your horse.

* **Promote science and the arts by giving inventors and authors exclusive rights to their respective discoveries and works (aka patents and copyrights).**
* **Establish federal courts under the Supreme Court.**

FYI

We'll elaborate in Article III, but the main levels of federal courts under the Supreme Court are district courts and circuit (aka appellate) courts. There are other federal courts like the Court of International Trade, the Foreign Intelligence Surveillance Court, and the Alien Terrorist Removal Court (a very chill name), but the ones to remember are district courts, circuit (aka appellate) courts, and the Supreme Court.

* **Define and punish piracies and felonies on water (kind of cool).**
* **Define and punish offenses against the law of nations (international law).**
* **Declare war.**

BTW

The last war that Congress actually declared was World War II (against 6 countries). Which means that the Korean War, the Vietnam War, the Persian Gulf War, the Bosnian War, the "War on Terror" (e.g., Afghanistan, Al Qaeda), the Iraq War, and other "wars" have not been declared by Congress, although it "authorized" those engagements. It seems like there's a weird, concerning pattern of entering wars without actually declaring them. Something fun to think about.

* **Grant letters of "marque and reprisal."**

FYI

In 1787, letters of marque and reprisal allowed ordinary citizens who owned ships to attack enemy ships and capture and plunder these ships, and then an admiralty court (for stuff that happened on water) would decide what they could keep (it's also called "privateering"). Although America doesn't do this anymore on principle, it's technically still possible for Congress to authorize this since the U.S. hasn't banned it or signed any prohibiting treaties. Although I don't know how intimidating it'd be for our enemies to see barefoot billionaires wandering their yachts or DJ Khaled doing figure 8s on his Jet Ski, but you get the idea.

> ✶ **Make the rules for capturing enemies on land or water.**
> ✶ **Authorize military budgets lasting 2 years at most.**
> ✶ **Finance the navy.**
> ✶ **Make the rules for governing and regulating the army and the navy.**
> ✶ **Finance the militia to help execute federal laws, stop uprisings, and block invasions.**
> ✶ **Finance and oversee the militia's organization, arming, and discipline.**
> ✶ **Govern whichever part of the militia is in use, although individual states can appoint their own militia officers and train their members with guidelines established by Congress.**

FYI

That is a lot. But the question is, what's a militia? This was first answered in the Militia Act of 1792, which clarified militia members as "free," "able-bodied," "white male" U.S. citizens living in the states between the ages of 18 and 44. The Militia Act of 1862 expanded this to include able-bodied males of all races between the ages of 18 and 44. Then the Militia Act of 1903 established the U.S. National Guard as the main military reserves in the country. And then in 1956, women were permitted to serve in the National Guard in a limited capacity, and in 2016 women could serve without limits (IN 2016). Anyway, that's where we're at with militias.

* **Establish and oversee the nation's capital, which must be 10 square miles at most.**

BTW

The first capital under the Constitution was New York City. This lasted a year. In 1790, Congress passed the Residence Act, choosing a plot of land on the Potomac River (now Washington, D.C.) to be the permanent capital. The deal was struck between Alexander Hamilton, Thomas Jefferson, and James Madison—Hamilton basically traded the national capital in exchange for Jefferson's and Madison's support in creating a national bank (play "The Room Where It Happens" on Spotify, Apple Music, YouTube, Amazon Music, SoundCloud—look, there are too many apps). The land was donated by Maryland and Virginia and called "Washington, District of Columbia," after George Washington and Christopher Columbus ("Columbia" was slang for "America" during the Revolutionary War). In 1800, Congress began operating from D.C. after a decade in Philadelphia, and it has been there ever since.

* **Own and oversee forts, magazines, arsenals, dockyards, and other government buildings, which Congress will build on the land that it buys from states <u>(with their legislatures' consent)</u>.**
* **Make laws for executing everything that the Constitution just listed, and any laws in general that regulate the federal government, its officers, and its departments.**

BTW

The Constitution says that Congress can make laws "necessary and proper" to do what it's allowed to do by the Constitution. But these laws aren't mentioned specifically, so whether or not a law is actually needed to enforce one of Congress's powers is debatable. For example, Congress can establish weights and measures. If Congress changed America to the metric system, and then threatened to revoke U.S. citizenship from anyone still using feet, you could argue this is enforcement related but unnecessary (and definitely a violation of the 8th Amendment, which we'll get to).

ARTICLE I: Section 9

The Migration or Importation of such Persons as any of the States now existing shall think proper to admit, shall not be prohibited by the Congress prior to the Year one thousand eight hundred and eight, but a Tax or duty may be imposed on such Importation, not exceeding ten dollars for each Person.

The Privilege of the Writ of Habeas Corpus shall not be suspended, unless when in Cases of Rebellion or Invasion the public Safety may require it.

No Bill of Attainder or ex post facto Law shall be passed.

No Capitation, or other direct, Tax shall be laid, unless in Proportion to the Census or enumeration herein before directed to be taken.

No Tax or Duty shall be laid on Articles exported from any State.

No Preference shall be given by any Regulation of Commerce or Revenue to the Ports of one State over those of another: nor shall Vessels bound to, or from, one State, be obliged to enter, clear, or pay Duties in another.

No Money shall be drawn from the Treasury, but in Consequence of Appropriations made by Law; and a regular Statement and Account of the Receipts and Expenditures of all public Money shall be published from time to time.

No Title of Nobility shall be granted by the United States: And no Person holding any Office of Profit or Trust under them, shall, without the Consent of the Congress, accept of any present, Emolument, Office, or Title, of any kind whatever, from any King, Prince, or foreign State.

ARTICLE I: SECTION 9
Congressional Limits
Here are some things that Congress *can't* do:

N/A

It's no longer relevant (thankfully), but Congress couldn't restrict the immigration or "importation" of people until 1808; it could impose a tax or a duty on "importation," but not more than $10 per person. This is a reference to slavery. The delegates gave themselves 20 years to import as many slaves as they wanted, with the compromise being that they might have to pay a tax on them. In return, the federal government couldn't ban America's participation in the international slave trade until 1808. And while President Jefferson championed banning the slave trade (which took effect January 1, 1808), he also owned 609 slaves during his life (more than any other president). I'm not saying that Jefferson didn't remove America from the international slave trade, because he did—but when you make something scarce, its value increases. And if you have a lot of it, then…yeah, I dunno, man.

⋆ **Suspend "habeas corpus," unless during a rebellion or an invasion.**

FYI

"Habeas corpus" gives you the right to see a judge, if you were arrested but you don't think you did anything wrong. At this point, the officers who detained you must either prove you were detained for a reason or let you go.

⋆ **Pass bills of attainder or ex post facto laws.**

FYI

A "bill of attainder" is a legislative act that punishes someone for a crime without giving them a trial. An "ex post facto law" means arresting someone for breaking a nonexistent law, establishing that law after the fact, and then retroactively charging them for breaking it. Which sounds super fucked up, but that's what was happening in England.

* Pass "capitations," or "direct" taxes, unless applicable to the whole population.

FYI

Capitations, or "poll taxes," are equal amounts of tax for everyone, like a "cost per head." We often hear about them in reference to voting, but the word "poll" doesn't mean polling places—it only means that the tax is the same for everyone to whom it applies. When you pay a fee to the government to register your car, get a hunting license, or renew your passport, those are sort of like poll taxes.

* Tax goods exported from one state to another.
* Give states preferential treatment over others in terms of commerce, especially when it comes to ports; also, ships owned by—or hailing from—one state can't be forced to enter, avoid, or pay duties to another (there's lots of ship stuff in here).
* Withdraw money from the U.S. treasury without Congress passing a law to approve the withdrawal. Congress must also publish a regular account of how it spends the public's money (i.e., our federal tax dollars).

IMO

I think Congress should publish a more frequent account of our federal tax spending, perhaps quarterly. It should be widely released, easily accessible, and clearly detailed. Congress not being held to account for its spending is part of why there is support for a balanced budget amendment among some state legislatures (we'll explain amendments in Article V). If you want to see how Congress spends our money, visit bit.ly/congressionalbudget (this is a link to the Congressional Budget Office website).

* Grant titles of nobility (king, queen, princess, etc.).
* Allow federal officials to accept gifts, money, offices, or titles from any person of nobility, foreign state, or foreign leader <u>without congressional approval.</u>

ARTICLE I: Section 10

No State shall enter into any Treaty, Alliance, or Confederation; grant Letters of Marque and Reprisal; coin Money; emit Bills of Credit; make any Thing but gold and silver Coin a Tender in Payment of Debts; pass any Bill of Attainder, ex post facto Law, or Law impairing the Obligation of Contracts, or grant any Title of Nobility.

No State shall, without the Consent of the Congress, lay any Imposts or Duties on Imports or Exports, except what may be absolutely necessary for executing it's inspection Laws: and the net Produce of all Duties and Imposts, laid by any State on Imports or Exports, shall be for the Use of the Treasury of the United States; and all such Laws shall be subject to the Revision and Controul of the Congress.

No State shall, without the Consent of Congress, lay any Duty of Tonnage, keep Troops, or Ships of War in time of Peace, enter into any Agreement or Compact with another State, or with a foreign Power, or engage in War, unless actually invaded, or in such imminent Danger as will not admit of delay.

ARTICLE I: SECTION 10

The Limits of States

Here are some things that the individual states *can't* do:

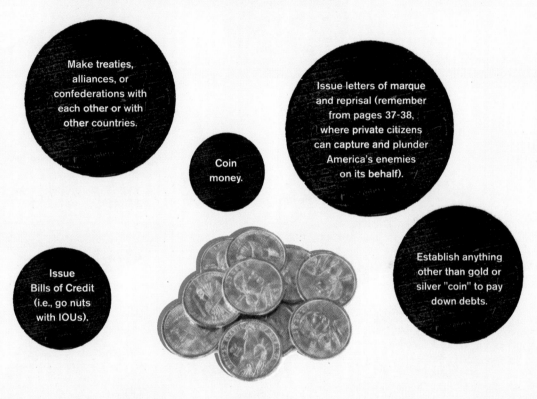

Make treaties, alliances, or confederations with each other or with other countries.

Issue letters of marque and reprisal (remember from pages 37-38, where private citizens can capture and plunder America's enemies on its behalf).

Coin money.

Issue Bills of Credit (i.e., go nuts with IOUs).

Establish anything other than gold or silver "coin" to pay down debts.

BTW

Regarding "debt," this was basically a way for Congress to prevent states from just making up their own currency, not backed by anything of value, and using it to pay down debts. If a bunch of states created their own currencies, it would be hard for them to do business with each other or the federal government.

Pass bills of attainder or ex post facto laws (that shady legal shit from earlier; see page 42).

Pass laws that invalidate contracts.

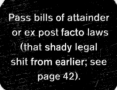

Establish duties and imposts (taxes on imports and exports) without congressional approval, except when the money is needed to fund inspections of imported goods (i.e., customs). And, even then, anything above what's needed for inspections goes to the federal government (the U.S. treasury) and not to the states. But Congress can change this whenever it wants.

Grant titles of nobility (they *hated* England).

Keep soldiers or warships during peacetime without congressional approval (this was to prevent states from arming themselves against other states or the federal government).

Charge commercial ships for entering, remaining in, or leaving a port without congressional approval (again with the ships).

Enter into agreements with other states, or foreign powers, without congressional approval.

Engage in war unless invaded—or in imminent danger of being invaded—without congressional approval.

Article I is dor

ARTICLE II: Section 1

The executive Power shall be vested in a President of the United States of America. He shall hold his Office during the Term of four Years, and, together with the Vice President, chosen for the same Term, be elected, as follows

Each State shall appoint, in such Manner as the Legislature thereof may direct, a Number of Electors, equal to the whole Number of Senators and Representatives to which the State may be entitled in the Congress: but no Senator or Representative, or Person holding an Office of Trust or Profit under the United States, shall be appointed an Elector.

The Electors shall meet in their respective States, and vote by Ballot for two Persons, of whom one at least shall not be an Inhabitant of the same State with themselves. And they shall make a List of all the Persons voted for, and of the Number of Votes for each; which List they shall sign and certify, and transmit sealed to the Seat of the Government of the United States, directed to the President of the Senate. The President of the Senate shall, in the Presence of the Senate and House of Representatives, open all the Certificates, and the Votes shall then be counted. The Person having the greatest Number of Votes shall be the President, if such Number be a Majority of the whole Number of Electors appointed; and if there be more than one who have such Majority, and have an equal Number of Votes, then the House of Representatives shall immediately chuse by Ballot one of them for President; and if no Person have a Majority, then from the five highest on the List the said House shall in like Manner chuse the President. But in chusing the President, the Votes shall be taken by States, the Representation from each State having one Vote; A quorum for this Purpose shall consist of a Member or Members from two thirds of the States, and a Majority of all the States shall be necessary to a Choice. In every Case, after the Choice of the President, the Person having the greatest Number of Votes of the Electors shall be the Vice President. But if there should remain two or more who have equal Votes, the Senate shall chuse from them by Ballot the Vice President.

The Congress may determine the Time of chusing the Electors, and the Day on which they shall give their Votes; which Day shall be the same throughout the United States.

No Person except a natural born Citizen, or a Citizen of the United States, at the time of the Adoption of this Constitution, shall be eligible to the Office of President; neither shall any Person be eligible to that Office who shall not have attained to the Age of thirty five Years, and been fourteen Years a Resident within the United States.

In Case of the Removal of the President from Office, or of his Death, Resignation, or Inability to discharge the Powers and Duties of the said Office, the Same shall devolve on the Vice President, and the Congress may by Law provide for the Case of Removal, Death, Resignation or Inability, both of the President and Vice President, declaring what Officer shall then act as President, and such Officer shall act accordingly, until the Disability be removed, or a President shall be elected.

The President shall, at stated Times, receive for his Services, a Compensation, which shall neither be encreased nor diminished during the Period for which he shall have been elected, and he shall not receive within that Period any other Emolument from the United States, or any of them.

Before he enter on the Execution of his Office, he shall take the following Oath or Affirmation:—"I do solemnly swear (or affirm) that I will faithfully execute the Office of President of the United States, and will to the best of my Ability, preserve, protect and defend the Constitution of the United States."

THE PRESIDENT (AKA THE EXECUTIVE BRANCH)
4 SECTIONS
ARTICLE II: SECTION 1
Electing and Paying the President

The president is the chief executive of the United States. The president and vice president serve the same 4-year term.

To choose the president and the vice president, each state's legislature picks its "electors," who will vote for them directly.

BTW

We didn't always vote for president; technically we still don't. Each state's legislature chooses how to pick its "electors," the people who will *directly* vote for president. Legislatures can allow voters to pick the state's electors, or they can choose the electors themselves, or use another method. It wasn't until 1880 that every state legislature stopped picking presidential electors and held a statewide popular vote instead (aka us going to the polls to vote for president). As for who can be an elector, the state's political parties usually choose loyalists who pledge to vote for that party's nominee. But as of this writing, electors *don't* have to vote for the statewide popular vote winner in 18 states. Throughout history there have been 167 "faithless" electors who didn't vote for whom they said they would, but those electoral votes never changed the outcome of an election. Anyway, when we vote for president we're actually just voting for a few people from our state who will directly vote for whomever wins our state's popular vote for president (except in Maine and Nebraska, but more on them later). What a clear and simple process.

The number of electors from each state equals its U.S. representatives (varies by state) plus its U.S. senators (always 2). The electors can't be the representatives or senators themselves, or any other federal officers.

BTW

This is the Electoral College, but "Electoral College" never appears in the Constitution. Also "college" means a group of people (i.e., the electors), not an actual school or university (if you get an email about enrolling in Electoral College classes, it's spam).

N/A

The next part of the Constitution was changed by the 12th Amendment; it describes how we *used* to pick presidents and vice presidents. The electors would meet in their state to vote for 2 people, at least one of whom couldn't live in that state. They'd write down names, and the votes each one got, and then sign and send the votes to the president of the Senate (aka the current vice president). Surrounded by Congress, the vice president would open and count the votes. If someone received a majority, they became the president. If a majority of votes was cast and 2 people tied, the House would immediately choose the president from those 2. If no one received a majority of electoral votes, the House would pick the president from the top 5 vote-getters. But when the House was voting, each *state* (not representative) would get a vote. At least ⅔ of states, with at least 1 representative from each state, were required, and a majority was needed to win. In each of these scenarios, whoever got the 2nd most votes became the vice president. If there was a tie for 2nd place, the Senate would pick the VP with a majority vote, where each senator would get 1 vote. Again, *simple*.

> **Congress decides when states should pick their electors, and on which day these electors must vote. This day must be the same for every state.**

BTW

We discussed Election Day before, but technically the Constitution *doesn't* say that voting for president (or "electors") needs to be on the same day as voting for representatives and senators in a presidential election year. To make it easier, we consolidate the elections on the same Tuesday after the 1st Monday in November because of the harvest (ridiculous). And since 1948, electors have cast their votes for president and vice president on the Monday after the 2nd Wednesday in December. I guess they had something against calendars with numbered days? I find this very weird.

The only requirements to be president are:

✶ **You must be a "natural born Citizen," or a U.S. citizen by the time the Constitution is adopted (so, by 1788).**
✶ **You must be at least 35 years old.**
✶ **You must have lived in the U.S. for at least 14 years.**
✶ **Nothing else.**

IMO

"Natural born" citizen is unclear. Does it mean born in the United States? What about born to U.S. citizens living abroad? What if you're born somewhere that later becomes a part of the U.S.? I know the delegates were trying to prevent a foreign national coming to America, living here for 14 years, becoming a citizen, turning 35, winning the presidency, and then selling out the country, but that's a pretty specific (and honestly creative) long game. In 2003, an amendment was proposed that would've allowed Arnold Schwarzenegger (born in Austria) to run, but it died in committee. Ted Cruz was born in Canada to a Cuban man and an American woman, and John McCain was born in the Panama Canal Zone under U.S. control, but most experts agree these scenarios qualify as "natural born." Anyway, it seems like "natural born" could use a clarifying amendment.

N/A

The next part of the Constitution was changed by the 25th Amendment, but it said that if the president was removed, died, resigned, or couldn't do the job, it would fall to the vice president. But if the vice president couldn't do the job either, Congress could pass a law establishing which federal officer should act as president until the president or the vice president could resume the job, or a new president could be elected. The takeaway here is that <u>Congress can decide the line of succession to the presidency</u>. As of 2006, the order has been the vice president, the speaker of the House, and the Senate president pro tempore—followed by the heads of all 15 executive (Cabinet) departments in their order of creation: secretary of state, secretary of the treasury, secretary of defense, attorney general, secretary of the interior, secretary of agriculture, secretary of commerce, secretary of labor, secretary of health and human services, secretary of housing and urban development, secretary of transportation, secretary of energy, secretary of education, secretary of veterans affairs, and secretary of homeland security. No offense to the secretary of homeland security, but if they were to become the acting president it would mean an absolutely horrific, insanely catastrophic series of events has just occurred.

The president earns a salary, which is paid out at specific times, and can't go up or down during their term. The president can't earn an additional salary, or salary equivalent, while in office—either from the federal government or from any state's government.

FYI

Since 2001, the president's annual salary has been $400,000.

Before officially becoming president, the president-elect (the winner of the election who has yet to be sworn in) must say the following words as an oath or affirmation: "I do solemnly swear (or affirm) that I [NAME] will faithfully execute the Office of President of the United States, and will to the best of my ability preserve, protect and defend the Constitution of the United States."

BTW

Some accounts say George Washington added "so help me God" after his first inauguration, but there's no documentation of it. Over the years some presidents have said it—and some haven't—but it isn't part of the constitutional oath.

PRESIDENTIAL LINE OF SUCCESSION

(Note: Department names have changed slightly over the years. Also, the below positions — except for the speaker and the president pro tempore — are in the Cabinet)

Vice President
Speaker of the House
Senate President Pro Tempore
Secretary of State (1789)
Secretary of the Treasury (1789)
Secretary of Defense (1789)
Attorney General (1789)
Secretary of the Interior (1849)
Secretary of Agriculture (1889)
Secretary of Commerce (1913)
Secretary of Labor (1913)
Secretary of Health and Human Services (1953)
Secretary of Housing and Urban Development (1965)
Secretary of Transportation (1966)
Secretary of Energy (1977)
Secretary of Education (1979)
Secretary of Veterans Affairs (1989)
Secretary of Homeland Security (2003)

Cabinet-level positions that don't succeed the president:

Administrator of the EPA (Environmental Protection Agency)
Administrator of the SBA (Small Business Administration)
Director of National Intelligence
Director of the CIA (Central Intelligence Agency)
Director of the Office of Management and Budget
U.S. Trade Representative
White House Chief of Staff

ARTICLE II: Section 2

The President shall be Commander in Chief of the Army and Navy of the United States, and of the Militia of the several States, when called into the actual Service of the United States; he may require the Opinion, in writing, of the principal Officer in each of the executive Departments, upon any Subject relating to the Duties of their respective Offices, and he shall have Power to grant Reprieves and Pardons for Offences against the United States, except in Cases of Impeachment.

He shall have Power, by and with the Advice and Consent of the Senate, to make Treaties, provided two thirds of the Senators present concur; and he shall nominate, and by and with the Advice and Consent of the Senate, shall appoint Ambassadors, other public Ministers and Consuls, Judges of the supreme Court, and all other Officers of the United States, whose Appointments are not herein otherwise provided for, and which shall be established by Law: but the Congress may by Law vest the

Appointment of such inferior Officers, as they think proper, in the President alone, in the Courts of Law, or in the Heads of Departments.

The President shall have Power to fill up all Vacancies that may happen during the Recess of the Senate, by granting Commissions which shall expire at the End of their next Session.

ARTICLE II: SECTION 2
Some of the President's Jobs

Whenever the U.S. Army, Navy, or militia (now the National Guard and Reserves) are called into service by Congress, the president is the commander in chief.

The president can request the written opinions of any executive department head on anything related to their department or job.

Here are some more things that the president can do:

* Grant reprieves (lessen punishments) or pardons (remove punishments) for federal crimes, *except* for impeachment.
* Make treaties with other countries—with the Senate's advice—as long as ⅔ of the senators in attendance approve.

BTW

The founders really prepared for when the representatives and senators just didn't show up to shit. In the 233 years since, this has been an apt prediction.

* Nominate ambassadors, ministers, consuls, Supreme Court justices, and other federal officers (whose roles aren't specifically mentioned), <u>as long as Congress creates those jobs by law</u>, and as long as the president gets the Senate's advice and approval on nominations.

- ✶ Appoint lower-level federal officers without Senate approval, <u>as long as Congress passes a law that allows this</u>; however, Congress can also give this ability to the courts, or to the executive department heads.
- ✶ Appoint federal officers if vacancies occur while the Senate is in recess (on a break), but the appointments only last until the end of the next Senate session.

ARTICLE II: Section 3

He shall from time to time give to the Congress Information of the State of the Union, and recommend to their Consideration such Measures as he shall judge necessary and expedient; he may, on extraordinary Occasions, convene both Houses, or either of them, and in Case of Disagreement between them, with Respect to the Time of Adjournment, he may adjourn them to such Time as he shall think proper; he shall receive Ambassadors and other public Ministers; he shall take Care that the Laws be faithfully executed, and shall Commission all the Officers of the United States.

ARTICLE II: SECTION 3

More of the President's Jobs

⭐ The president must occasionally give Congress a "state of
the union" (a report), and can suggest things for Congress
to consider that are necessary and timely.

BTW

There's no rule in the Constitution for how often the "state of the union"
must be; also, the Constitution doesn't say it needs to be a speech.
George Washington and John Adams gave speeches, and then every
president from Thomas Jefferson through William Howard Taft (a century's
worth) sent letters to be read aloud to Congress. Starting again with
Woodrow Wilson, presidents returned to giving speeches at the start of
the year.

* On extraordinary occasions (when shit's going down) the president can convene all of Congress, or just the House or the Senate. If the 2 chambers can't agree on when to adjourn, the president can decide for them.
* The president receives ambassadors and other public ministers.
* The president oversees the implementation of all federal laws in good faith (i.e., even if the president doesn't agree with the laws).
* The president commissions federal officers.

BTW

This sounds boring, but it changed the Supreme Court forever. In 1801, President John Adams—with the Senate's help—made several last-minute appointments to anger the incoming president, Thomas Jefferson. But when Jefferson took office, he learned that *some* of the appointment certificates hadn't been delivered, so he told his secretary of state, James Madison (all these dudes just swapped each other's positions, it was very incestuous), *not* to deliver the certificates, so the appointments would be void. In short, one of the guys who didn't get his certificate—William Marbury—sued. It led to an 1803 Supreme Court case that established the idea of "judicial review," where the Supreme Court can strike down laws it thinks are unconstitutional. Ever since, we've all assumed judicial review to be the Supreme Court's job, but it actually isn't in the Constitution. Anyway, Marbury didn't get his appointment, but the outcome is less important than the precedent his case established.

ARTICLE II: Section 4

The President, Vice President and all civil Officers of
the United States, shall be removed from Office on
Impeachment for, and Conviction of, Treason, Bribery, or
other high Crimes and Misdemeanors.

ARTICLE II: SECTION 4
Impeachment and Removal

The president, the vice president, and all other federal civil officers (of the executive or judicial branch—but not of the military or, since 1799, the legislative branch) must be removed by the Senate after being impeached by the House if convicted of treason (betraying America), bribery (selling out America), or other high crimes and misdemeanors (vague).

FYI

According to the House, "high crimes and misdemeanors" includes abuse of power and obstruction of Congress (Trump's impeachment), perjury and obstruction of justice (Clinton's impeachment), and abuse of power and contempt of Congress (Nixon's almost-impeachment, but his also included obstruction of justice). Andrew Johnson, the only other president besides Trump and Clinton to have been impeached, tried to replace the secretary of war (a job that no longer exists) without Senate approval in violaton of the Tenure of Office Act (a law that no longer exists). In short, of the presidential impeachments in history so far, one was for attempting to replace a then-Cabinet official without Senate approval, one was for attempting to pressure a foreign government to influence a U.S. presidential election, and the other was for lying under oath about a blowjob. Point is, "high crimes and misdemeanors" has a spectrum.

Article II is through.

ARTICLE III: Section 1

The judicial Power of the United States, shall be vested in one supreme Court, and in such inferior Courts as the Congress may from time to time ordain and establish. The Judges, both of the supreme and inferior Courts, shall hold their Offices during good Behaviour, and shall, at stated Times, receive for their Services, a Compensation, which shall not be diminished during their Continuance in Office.

THE SUPREME COURT (AKA THE JUDICIAL BRANCH) 3 SECTIONS
ARTICLE III: SECTION 1
Federal Judiciary Overview

The U.S. Supreme Court is the highest court in the country. Congress can establish other federal courts beneath it.

BTW

The Constitution doesn't say how many justices must be on the Supreme Court. In 1869, Congress set the number at 9, and it could pass a law tomorrow to change it. Also, there are no requirements to be a Supreme Court justice (semantics-wise, judges hear initial cases while justices hear appeals). Like with the speaker of the House and the Senate president pro tempore, anyone can be a Supreme Court justice. As long as the process for nominations and confirmations is followed, the next 4 justices could be every judge from *The Masked Singer*, leaving CBS as the only major network without a reality show running the country.

FYI

Here's a brief overview of the federal court system. There is 1 Supreme Court with 9 justices (1 chief, 8 associates), 13 circuit (aka appellate) courts with 179 judges total, and 94 district courts with 673 judges total (as of this writing). The numbers change because of vacancies and appointments, but that's roughly where we are. As mentioned, there are also special federal courts like the Court of International Trade (with 9 judges), U.S. bankruptcy courts, and that chill Alien Terrorist Removal Court, but you just need to know about Supreme, circuit (appellate), and district.

For district courts, circuit courts, the Supreme Court, and the Court of International Trade, justices and judges serve as long as they exhibit "good behavior," which basically means for life unless they quit or get impeached and removed.

BTW

The idea behind life appointments was to have judges' decisions be separate from party whims. But recently, constitutional scholars have proposed terms of 18 years—instead of life—to give judges less everlasting power.

BTW

Regarding impeachment, as of this writing there have been 20 federal impeachments in U.S. history. Fifteen have been judges (the most recent in 2010), and of the 8 federal officials who have been impeached *and* removed, all were either justices or judges (see the list at bit.ly/listofimpeachments; again, it's just the Senate's website).

Justices and judges earn a salary, which can't be lowered during their time in office.

ARTICLE III: Section 2

The judicial Power shall extend to all Cases, in Law and Equity, arising under this Constitution, the Laws of the United States, and Treaties made, or which shall be made, under their Authority;—to all Cases affecting Ambassadors, other public Ministers and Consuls;—to all Cases of admiralty and maritime Jurisdiction;—to Controversies to which the United States shall be a Party;—to Controversies between two or more States;—between a State and Citizens of another State,—between Citizens of different States,—between Citizens of the same State claiming Lands under Grants of different States, and between a State, or the Citizens thereof, and foreign States, Citizens or Subjects.

In all Cases affecting Ambassadors, other public Ministers and Consuls, and those in which a State shall be Party, the supreme Court shall have original Jurisdiction. In all the other Cases before mentioned, the supreme Court shall have appellate Jurisdiction, both as to Law and Fact, with such Exceptions, and under such Regulations as the Congress shall make.

The Trial of all Crimes, except in Cases of Impeachment, shall be by Jury; and such Trial shall be held in the State where the said Crimes shall have been committed; but when not committed within any State, the Trial shall be at such Place or Places as the Congress may by Law have directed.

ARTICLE III: SECTION 2

Federal Jurisdiction

Federal courts handle cases around federal laws, U.S. treaties, and the U.S. Constitution. They also handle cases affecting ambassadors, ministers, and consuls, and disputes that occur on sea (if we've learned anything it's to watch your back on these seas). Federal courts also handle cases where the U.S. is a plaintiff or a defendant, disputes between 2 or more states, disputes between citizens of different states, or disputes between citizens of one state arguing over land in different states (aka rich people problems).

N/A

This is a boring one, but the federal judiciary used to handle cases between a state and citizens of another state, as well as cases between a state (or its citizens) and a foreign country (or its citizens or subjects). This was changed by the 11th Amendment, which at face value is the worst amendment (we'll get to it later).

When ambassadors, ministers, consuls, or states are a party in the dispute, the case begins in the Supreme Court. But every other federal case begins elsewhere and can be appealed to the Supreme Court, although Congress can change which types of cases can be appealed to it.

Besides impeachment, trials are decided by jury and held in the state where the crime(s) were committed. If a crime wasn't committed in a state (i.e., a territory), the trial happens wherever Congress, by law, says it should.

BTW

Here is a general rule of thumb courtesy of a criminal prosecutor who would like to remain anonymous. They told me a crime committed fully in one state is a state crime. If a crime involves multiple states, referred to as affecting "interstate commerce," regardless of how loose the multi-state involvement is (e.g., an armed robbery committed in one state by a resident of that state, but the gun used was manufactured in a different state), it becomes a federal crime. This is because the delegates thought states could handle crimes that only impacted that state, but if crimes involved multiple states, the federal government had to intervene. And since federal sentences are harsher than state sentences, if you're going to commit a crime—BUT I DO NOT RECOMMEND THAT YOU DO—try to keep it fully within *one* state. But again, I can't stress this enough: DON'T DO CRIMES.

ARTICLE III: Section 3

Treason against the United States, shall consist only in levying War against them, or in adhering to their Enemies, giving them Aid and Comfort. No Person shall be convicted of Treason unless on the Testimony of two Witnesses to the same overt Act, or on Confession in open Court.

The Congress shall have Power to declare the Punishment of Treason, but no Attainder of Treason shall work Corruption of Blood, or Forfeiture except during the Life of the Person attainted.

ARTICLE III: SECTION 3

Treason

"Treason" is defined as waging war against America or obeying/helping its enemies in some fashion. You can only be convicted of treason if at least 2 people witnessed the same treasonous act, or if you decide to confess in open (aka public) court, which would be a bad idea.

Congress can set the punishment for treason, but it can only apply to you and not to your future descendants. The punishment for treason can't affect your estate after you die.

BTW

It's obvious that treason was the worst thing you could do in 1787, so a big takeaway from the Constitution is to not do treason.

Article III may go free.

ARTICLE IV: Section 1

Full Faith and Credit shall be given in each State to the public Acts, Records, and judicial Proceedings of every other State. And the Congress may by general Laws prescribe the Manner in which such Acts, Records and Proceedings shall be proved, and the Effect thereof.

THE STATES
4 SECTIONS
ARTICLE IV: Section 1

States Must Respect Other States

States must respect each other's laws, records, and judicial processes (e.g., verdicts, court orders, punishments) even if they are—or would be—different from their own. <u>Congress can also make laws establishing how states recognize and honor each other's laws, records, and judicial processes.</u>

ARTICLE IV: Section 2

The Citizens of each State shall be entitled to all Privileges and Immunities of Citizens in the several States.

A Person charged in any State with Treason, Felony, or other Crime, who shall flee from Justice, and be found in another State, shall on Demand of the executive Authority of the State from which he fled, be delivered up, to be removed to the State having Jurisdiction of the Crime.

No Person held to Service or Labour in one State, under the Laws thereof, escaping into another, shall, in Consequence of any Law or Regulation therein, be discharged from such Service or Labour, but shall be delivered up on Claim of the Party to whom such Service or Labour may be due.

ARTICLE IV: SECTION 2
Equal States and Fleeing States

States can't deny to other states' citizens the rights and protections they allow to their *own* citizens (i.e., North Dakota can't discriminate against South Dakotans).

If someone flees a state after committing treason, felony, or another crime, and is found in another state, the governor of the state where the crime happened can demand the person be returned (presumably for trial).

BTW

If someone committed a crime and fled to another state, and instead of law enforcement some random person found the criminal, captured them without a warrant, tied them up, and returned them to the state where the crime occurred, the criminal can stand trial even though their detention was *wildly* illegal. If you think about this, it's kind of how Batman operates (don't think about it too much).

N/A

This part no longer applies because slavery no longer exists, but it said that slaves and indentured servants who fled from one state to another must be returned to their masters in the state from which they fled, regardless of whether the state they ended up in permitted slavery. Another fucked-up part of the Constitution rendered irrelevant by the 13th Amendment.

ARTICLE IV: Section 3

New States may be admitted by the Congress into this Union; but no new State shall be formed or erected within the Jurisdiction of any other State; nor any State be formed by the Junction of two or more States, or Parts of States, without the Consent of the Legislatures of the States concerned as well as of the Congress.

The Congress shall have Power to dispose of and make all needful Rules and Regulations respecting the Territory or other Property belonging to the United States; and nothing in this Constitution shall be so construed as to Prejudice any Claims of the United States, or of any particular State.

ARTICLE IV: SECTION 3

New States and Federal Property

New states must be approved by Congress. States can't be created within an existing state, or by merging 2 or more states, or by merging parts of 2 or more states <u>without approval from Congress and those states' legislatures</u> (i.e., Congress can't break the Carolinas into more Carolinas without the Carolinas' permission).

Congress has the power to relinquish U.S. territories and properties, and to make the rules regarding them (according to a 1901 Supreme Court case, this includes deciding which parts of the Constitution apply to them). Nothing in the Constitution can be used to negatively influence land disputes, whether the land in question is federal or state property.

FYI

"Property" includes things like national parks, national forests, and wildlife refuges, and the land used for federal buildings and military bases. As of 2017, 28 percent of the land in the U.S. is owned by the federal government, including more than half of Alaska, Idaho, Oregon, and Utah and 80 PERCENT OF NEVADA (of *course* the state with the most legal gambling and prostitution has the highest share of government ownership).

FYI

"Territory," remember from the intro, refers to land that isn't a part of the continental United States and isn't a state.

IMO

I strongly believe that Puerto Rico should be a state. Puerto Ricans have voted 5 times on statehood—1967 (39 percent "yes" with 66 percent turnout), 1993 (47 percent "yes" with

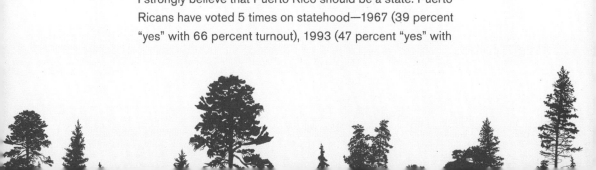

74 percent turnout), 1998 (47 percent "yes" with 71 percent turnout), 2012 (61 percent "yes" with 78 percent turnout), and 2017 (97 percent "yes" with 23 percent turnout, because of protests over the ballot's wording). In 2017, an *El Nuevo Día* poll had 52 percent of Puerto Ricans supporting statehood. Puerto Ricans also pay federal taxes; in Fiscal 2018 (October 1, 2017, to September 30, 2018) the island paid $3.4 billion in federal tax. Puerto Rico has a higher population than 21 states and a higher population than Wyoming, Vermont, Alaska, and North Dakota combined. But Puerto Rico has 0 U.S. senators, 1 non-voting U.S. representative, and 0 electoral votes for president and vice president. Former presidents Gerald Ford, Ronald Reagan, and George H. W. Bush openly supported statehood—and Bill Clinton, George W. Bush, and Barack Obama said the island should decide. In June 2019, 66 percent of Americans supported Puerto Rican statehood. But in 2015, 2017, and 2018, bills that would've granted statehood died in committee. In 2019 (as of this writing), another House bill has been introduced. It's ridiculous that Congress won't let 3.3 million U.S. citizens have a voice in a government they help pay for, which includes the salaries and expenses of the members of Congress who are denying them statehood. I'd argue that the other 4 territories, with 377,000 taxpayers, should have some level of voting representation too, as well as Washington, D.C. (which we'll get to later). But in terms of population and taxes, Puerto Rico is an outlier. It's billions of dollars annually in taxation without representation. So in short, Congress should get off its ass and make Puerto Rico a state.

ARTICLE IV: Section 4

The United States shall guarantee to every State in this Union a Republican Form of Government, and shall protect each of them against Invasion; and on Application of the Legislature, or of the Executive (when the Legislature cannot be convened), against domestic Violence.

ARTICLE IV: SECTION 4
State Governments and Federal Protections

Like the U.S. itself, each state is also a republic (remember from page 9, where the people elect representatives to govern on their behalf). The U.S. will protect each state from foreign invasion and from domestic threats *if* the state legislature asks. If the state legislature can't meet, the governor can ask for this protection.

Article IV is no more.

ARTICLE V

The Congress, whenever two thirds of both Houses shall deem it necessary, shall propose Amendments to this Constitution, or, on the Application of the Legislatures of two thirds of the several States, shall call a Convention for proposing Amendments, which, in either Case, shall be valid to all Intents and Purposes, as Part of this Constitution, when ratified by the Legislatures of three fourths of the several States, or by Conventions in three fourths thereof, as the one or the other Mode of Ratification may be proposed by the Congress; Provided that no Amendment which may be made prior to the Year One thousand eight hundred and eight shall in any Manner affect the first and fourth Clauses in the Ninth Section of the first Article; and that no State, without its Consent, shall be deprived of its equal Suffrage in the Senate.

THE ADMENDMENT PROCESS
ARTICLE V
Amending the Constitution

Constitutional amendments must be proposed by ⅔ of the House and the Senate, *or* at a constitutional convention called for by ⅔ of state legislatures (34). To ratify an amendment, ¾ (38) of state legislatures *or* of states holding constitutional conventions are required. <u>Congress can pick whichever ratification method it wants.</u>

BTW

Almost 12,000 amendments have been proposed in Congress, but only 33 have been sent to the states (of which 27 were ratified).

N/A

Two of the unratified 6—the Equal Rights Amendment (equal rights for citizens regardless of sex) and the D.C. Voting Rights Amendment (full congressional representation, Electoral College representation, and full participation in the amendment process)—expired in 1979 and 1985. But for the ERA specifically, there has been a resurgence of ratifications despite its 1979 expiration (and disputed 1982 extension). Prior to 1979, 35 states had ratified the ERA. Three states—Nevada, Illinois, and Virginia—recently ratified it in 2017, 2018, and 2020, giving it the ¾ of states necessary to enter the Constitution. But there are issues. First, there is a dispute over whether Congress can actually repeal the expiration date; one argument for this is that the expiration isn't in the amendment's text, only its preamble (even individual amendments got preambles in the '70s). There's also the issue that as many as 5 states have rescinded their ratifications, which is something the Constitution doesn't specifically address. Point is, as of this writing, the ERA has re-emerged as a hot-button issue, but regardless of how you feel about it (personally, I support it), there are many unanswered questions around its viability.

FYI

Four of the unratified 6 are still alive. The 1st was proposed along with the Bill of Rights in 1789, establishing the number of constituents each U.S. representative would have when the House reached 100 and 200 members (we now have 435 members, so this is moot). The 2nd, from 1810, revokes U.S. citizenship and the ability to hold federal office from people who accept titles of nobility, or gifts from a foreign power, <u>without congressional permission</u>. The 3rd, from 1861, prevents Congress from interfering with states' affairs, including slavery (which was banned 4 years later, so this is moot too). And the 4th, from 1926, allows Congress to regulate child labor laws for people under age 18. Also, every one of those 33 proposed amendments was done so via Congress; the other method where 2/3 of states can call for a constitutional convention to propose amendments has never happened.

N/A

This no longer applies since we're post-1808, but there couldn't be an amendment affecting the migration of people—or really, the importation of slaves—until 1808. Before then there also couldn't be an amendment making direct (aka poll) taxes apply to some, and not all, of the population.

Lastly, there can't be an amendment that changes the rule of states getting equal votes in the Senate (2 per state), and that states can opt out of equal votes in the Senate if they want.

BTW

This would be weird to do, and would probably lead to state legislators losing their jobs. But the strangest part about this section is that because the other protected section (about slaves and taxes pre-1808) has expired, this odd part about states being able to opt out of equal Senate votes is THE ONLY PART OF THE CONSTITUTION SHIELDED FROM AN AMENDMENT. Some experts think you could pass an amendment to remove the shield, and another to remove the rule, but if the delegates thought this was possible then why include a non-amendable clarification at all? I guess it doesn't matter because no state would do this, but of all the things to shield, it's a weird one.

Article V is no longer alive.

ARTICLE VI

All Debts contracted and Engagements entered into, before the Adoption of this Constitution, shall be as valid against the United States under this Constitution, as under the Confederation.

This Constitution, and the Laws of the United States which shall be made in Pursuance thereof; and all Treaties made, or which shall be made, under the Authority of the United States, shall be the supreme Law of the Land; and the Judges in every State shall be bound thereby, any Thing in the Constitution or Laws of any State to the Contrary notwithstanding.

The Senators and Representatives before mentioned, and the Members of the several State Legislatures, and all executive and judicial Officers, both of the United States and of the several States, shall be bound by Oath or Affirmation, to support this Constitution; but no religious Test shall ever be required as a Qualification to any Office or public Trust under the United States.

FOLLOWING THE CONSTITUTION
ARTICLE VI
You Must Follow this Constitution and We Can't Require a National Religion

All debts and IOUs that existed before the Constitution, when the country was just a collection of independent states, still exist under this Constitution.

This Constitution, future federal laws, and existing and future treaties apply to *all* states, territories, and properties, and the judges in each state must follow them regardless of each state's own constitution or laws (or in other words, federal law trumps state law).

All U.S. representatives, U.S. senators, state legislators, and executive and judicial officers at the federal *and* the state level must adhere to this Constitution either by oath (religious) or affirmation (non-religious).

Finally, no religious test can ever be required for someone to hold federal office.

Article VI was quick.

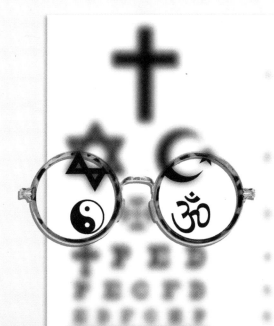

ARTICLE VII

The Ratification of the Conventions of nine States, shall be sufficient for the Establishment of this Constitution between the States so ratifying the Same.

The Word, "the," being interlined between the seventh and eighth Lines of the first Page, The Word "Thirty" being partly written on an Erazure in the fifteenth Line of the first Page, The Words "is tried" being interlined between the thirty second and thirty third Lines of the first Page and the Word "the" being interlined between the forty third and forty fourth Lines of the second Page.

Attest William Jackson Secretary

done in Convention by the Unanimous Consent of the States present the Seventeenth Day of September in the Year of our Lord one thousand seven hundred and Eighty seven and of the Independance of the United States of America the Twelfth In witness whereof We have hereunto subscribed our Names,

G°. Washington

Presidt and deputy from Virginia

ARTICLE VII
We Did It ☺

As soon as 9 state conventions ratify this Constitution, which we finished writing and editing on September 17, 1787, it will take effect.

BTW

Of the 41 delegates present at signing, 3 refused to sign—Elbridge Gerry, George Mason, and Edmund Randolph. There were actually only 38 signers present, but George Read signed it on behalf of John Dickinson, who was sick, to make it 39. The 9 states that ratified the Constitution were Delaware (December 7, 1787), Pennsylvania (December 12, 1787), New Jersey (December 18, 1787), Georgia (January 2, 1788), Connecticut (January 9, 1788), Massachusetts (February 6, 1788), Maryland (April 28, 1788), South Carolina (May 23, 1788), and New Hampshire (June 21, 1788). They were followed by Virginia (June 25, 1788), New York (July 26, 1788), North Carolina (November 21, 1789), and Rhode Island (May 29, 1790). In addition to being the last to ratify, Rhode Island was also the only state to completely skip the convention. Not saying it's a curse, but to this day—land-wise—it's the smallest state (I mean, 430 Rhode Islands could fit inside Alaska).

Article VII is in heaven.

THE STATES THAT RATIFIED THE CONSTITUTION, IN ORDER, WERE:

Delaware December 7, 1787	South Carolina May 23, 1788
Pennsylvania December 12, 1787	New Hampshire* June 21, 1788
New Jersey December 18, 1787	Virginia June 25, 1788
Georgia January 2, 1788	New York July 26, 1788
Connecticut January 9, 1788	North Carolina November 21, 1789
Massachusetts February 6, 1788	Rhode Island May 29, 1790
Maryland April 28, 1788	*Officially ratified

LETTER OF TRANSMITTAL

In Convention Monday September 17th 1787.
Present The States of New Hampshire, Massachusetts,
Connecticut, Mr. Hamilton from New York, New Jersey,
Pennsylvania, Delaware, Maryland, Virginia, North
Carolina, South Carolina and Georgia.

Resolved, That the proceeding Constitution be laid before
the United States in Congress assembled, and that it is the
Opinion of this Convention, that it should afterwards be
submitted to a Convention of Delegates, chosen in each State
by the People thereof, under the Recommendation of its
Legislature, for their Assent and Ratification; and that each
Convention assenting to, and ratifying the Same, should give
Notice thereof to the United States in Congress assembled.

Resolved, That it is the Opinion of this Convention,
that as soon as the Conventions of nine States shall have
ratified this Constitution, the United States in Congress
assembled should fix a Day on which Electors should be
appointed by the States which shall have ratified the same,

and a Day on which the Electors should assemble to vote for the President, and the Time and Place for commencing Proceedings under this Constitution.

That after such Publication the Electors should be appointed, and the Senators and Representatives elected: That the Electors should meet on the Day fixed for the Election of the President, and should transmit their Votes certified, signed, sealed and directed, as the Constitution requires, to the Secretary of the United States in Congress assembled, that the Senators and Representatives should convene at the Time and Place assigned; that the Senators should appoint a President of the Senate, for the sole Purpose of receiving, opening and counting the Votes for President; and, that after he shall be chosen, the Congress, together with the President, should, without Delay, proceed to execute this Constitution.

By the unanimous Order of the Convention

G. WASHINGTON--Presidt.

W. JACKSON Secretary.

WE ALSO WROTE A LETTER

This Constitution should be presented to Congress, and then sent to the states, where each state will have its own convention. The people of each state will choose the delegates for these conventions however their state legislature decides. If a state wants to ratify, it should let Congress know. As soon as 9 states ratify, Congress should pick a day when the ratifying states' electors—chosen by the states—can assemble to vote for president. Congress should also pick a time and a place for us to start governing.

When the electors are chosen, and the senators and representatives are elected, the electors will then meet on the specified day and time to vote for president and then send those votes to Congress, which will also meet at a specific time/place. The senators will choose the president of the Senate who will count the votes for president. When the president is decided, both Congress and the new president can start doing shit.

Sincerely,

George Washington, president of the Constitutional Convention

William Jackson, secretary of the Constitutional Convention

THE AMENDMENTS

There are 27 amendments to the U.S. Constitution; the first 10 are called "The Bill of Rights." The Bill of Rights was written by James Madison, which brings me to something I've been wanting to share...

If we're being honest, James Madison is the real founder of this country. He wrote the first draft of the Constitution (aka the Virginia Plan, the first one presented at the convention), which had the legislative, executive, and judicial branches mapped out with checks and balances. Madison was such a devoted note-taker and participant—the "director" of the convention (Washington was its president, but he actually didn't want to be there)—to the point that he's called the "Father of the Constitution." After the Constitution was written, Madison and 2 others wrote *The Federalist Papers* (aka the Constitution's marketing plan), with Madison writing 29 of its 85 essays (John Jay wrote 5 and Alexander Hamilton wrote 51; if you knew that, congrats on being a theater nerd). Then, during the ratification debate, some delegates still had concerns about the federal government's power, so Madison wrote 19 amendments in exchange for those delegates' votes on the Constitution. Madison proposed the amendments to Congress on June 8, 1789, and called them the "great rights of mankind" (something a great founder would do). The House liked 17, and sent those to the Senate. The Senate liked 12, so Congress sent those to the states. The states ratified 10, and these became the Bill of Rights. And then 203 years later, one of the 2 amendments that was sent to the states but *not* ratified became the 27th Amendment. So to recap, James Madison—a Virginia delegate at the Constitutional Convention—wrote the first draft of the Constitution that everyone went off of. He was so active at the convention that he's called the Constitution's "father." He wrote 34 percent of its marketing and 41 percent of its amendments. He was also a U.S. representative from Virginia, an adviser to

President Washington, U.S. secretary of state under President Jefferson, and president himself for 8 years. But Madison has no coins, current bills, or monuments; isn't on Mount Rushmore; and doesn't have a single Hollywood biopic or TV show about him. John Adams didn't even attend the convention and he got an HBO miniseries with fucking Paul Giamatti. In exchange for designing our government and enumerating our rights Madison got...a library wing and a school that can't play in bowl games. In terms of strikes against him, while Madison was privately against slavery, he did own more than 100 slaves and didn't free them in his will. He also proposed the ⅗ compromise. But in context, George Washington had more than 300 slaves and Thomas Jefferson had more than 600 slaves, including TWO OF HIS OWN KIDS THAT HE FATHERED WITH A TEENAGER THAT HE OWNED— and those guys have prime D.C. real estate. I kind of wonder if the founders' posthumous fame just came down to whether they landed on current money and whether they look good in portraits. For Madison, it's "no" and "not really," and that's a shame.

Anyway, here are the amendments.

Preamble

Congress of the United States begun and held at the City of New-York, on Wednesday the fourth of March, one thousand seven hundred and eighty nine.

THE Conventions of a number of the States, having at the time of their adopting the Constitution, expressed a desire, in order to prevent misconstruction or abuse of its powers, that further declaratory and restrictive clauses should be added: And as extending the ground of public confidence in the Government, will best ensure the beneficent ends of its institution.

RESOLVED by the Senate and House of Representatives of the United States of America, in Congress assembled, two thirds of both Houses concurring, that the following Articles be proposed to the Legislatures of the several States, as amendments to the Constitution of the United States, all, or any of which Articles, when ratified by three fourths of the said Legislatures, to be valid to all intents and purposes, as part of the said Constitution; viz.

ARTICLES in addition to, and Amendment of the Constitution of the United States of America, proposed by Congress, and ratified by the Legislatures of the several States, pursuant to the fifth Article of the original Constitution.

PREAMBLE
September 25, 1789

Congress knows the ratifying states are still concerned about the Constitution; mainly, that the federal government might abuse its power. So Congress is sending these amendments, approved by ⅔ of its members in the House and the Senate, to the state legislatures. As Article V says, if ¾ of state legislatures vote to ratify these amendments, they become part of the U.S. Constitution.

Best,

Frederick Augustus Muhlenberg, Speaker of the House of Representatives

John Adams, President of the Senate (also Vice President)

CC: John Beckley, Clerk of the House of Representatives

CC: Sam A. Otis, Secretary of the Senate

Amendment I

Congress shall make no law respecting an establishment of religion, or prohibiting the free exercise thereof; or abridging the freedom of speech, or of the press; or the right of the people peaceably to assemble, and to petition the Government for a redress of grievances.

1ST AMENDMENT

You may express yourself freely without consequence.

Ratified December 15, 1791

Congress can't make a law establishing a religion, banning a religion, preventing free speech, preventing free press, stopping people from assembling peacefully, or punishing people for complaining about their government, even to their government.

BTW

Since 1791, the Supreme Court has decided the amendment *doesn't* shield things like inciting violence or harmful situations (e.g., falsely yelling "fire" in a theater), slander (defamatory speech), libel (defamatory writing or imagery), obscenity (which is vague), child pornography (which is pretty specific), false advertising, intellectual property violations (of copyrights, trademarks, patents), and more.

Also, this amendment applies specifically to Congress, then later to the state legislatures (via the 14th Amendment, which we'll get to); it does not apply to private companies or individuals. When it comes to free speech and free press, companies like Facebook (including Instagram), Alphabet (including YouTube), Twitter, and Snapchat are not bound by the 1st Amendment. If they want to limit speech on their platforms, they can (and they do).

Amendment II

A well regulated Militia, being necessary to the security of a free State, the right of the people to keep and bear Arms, shall not be infringed.

2ND AMENDMENT

You can own/use guns...in a militia ...?

Ratified December 15, 1791

A well-regulated militia is necessary for the security of a free country; as such, the country's people can have and use weapons and ammo.

IMO

The 2nd Amendment is probably the most debated amendment today. But there have only been 6 cases directly affecting it in the Supreme Court (although as of this writing, there's another case pending). I'm not a lawyer, nor a Supreme Court justice (but I could be: there are no requirements), and I don't intend to solve this debate here (there are whole books dedicated to it). So I can just share how it appears to me, having read this Constitution more times than I honestly ever thought I would.

To start, "free state" means "free country" and not "free individual state." In the Constitution's 7 articles, "Militia" is mentioned twice: Article I, Section 8 and Article II, Section 2. Each time, "Militia" refers to a supplemental army to the U.S. Army. Article I, Section 8 says that it's Congress's job to organize, arm, discipline, govern, and set training for the militia, and Article II, Section 2 says that the president is the commander in chief of the militia when it is called into service. So it's clear that the militia is federal. The only rights that states get with the militia, according to the Constitution, are that they can choose their own officers and train their own members with programs established by Congress. Also, as mentioned earlier, the militia is now basically the National Guard and Reserves.

But now the big questions: What does "well-regulated" mean? Are we talking about all people or just militia members? And what does "infringed" actually mean? Again, my opinion, but the Constitution says that Congress organizes, arms, disciplines, governs, and establishes training for the militia. So it's pretty clear that

Congress regulates the militia. Clearly, a militia doesn't exist without its members, who were first defined as "free," "able-bodied," "white male" U.S. citizens living in the states between the ages of 18 and 44—and then as males of any race between 18 and 44—and then as basically anyone who's eligible for the National Guard and Reserves, including women in an unlimited capacity as of 2016 (nuts). As of this writing, the National Guard has these requirements on its website:

Joining without prior service:

* Be between the ages of 17 and 35.
* Be a U.S. citizen or permanent resident.
* Be at least a junior in high school, or have a high school diploma or a GED certificate.
* Achieve a minimum score on the ASVAB test.
  "The ASVAB is the Armed Services Vocational Aptitude Battery. It is an aptitude test that measures developed abilities and helps predict future academic and occupational success."
* Meet medical, physical, and moral requirements.

Joining with prior service:

* Be between 17 and 59, qualifying for non-regular retired pay by age 60.
* Meet height/weight and current medical requirements.
* Meet education standards for the MOS (military occupational specialties) or option for which you enlist.
* Have most current DD 214, NGB22, or discharge order and have an approved DD Form 368 Conditional Release.
* Potentially be required to attend a 6-week Basic Combat Training (BCT) course at Fort Leonard Wood, depending on the length of your break in service.

✭ With a break in service of over 10 years, you
   must re-take the ASVAB and get a current
   minimum score.

So whether or not you actually want to join the National Guard, as
long as you meet the basic requirements for no-prior-service or prior-
service members, then I think the Constitution protects your right to own
weapons and ammo. As far as "infringe" goes, if you meet the National
Guard requirements, then the federal government can't stand in the way
of you getting weapons or ammo. That's my honest attempt at interpreting
this amendment based on the founding documents.

But in 2008, the Supreme Court interpreted an individual's right to
own weapons and ammunition unconnected to either militia service or
eligibility. And in 2010, the Supreme Court said that interpretation also
applies to state and local governments (via the 14th Amendment). In 2016,
it said the amendment applies to all weapons, reversing a 1939 decision.
So regardless of your opinion, it's interesting that there have only been
6 Supreme Court decisions directly affecting the 2nd Amendment since
1875, but half of those have been since 2008 with another pending
(as of this writing). So, in other words, it has been a busy time for 2nd
Amendment cases as of late.

Amendment III

No Soldier shall, in time of peace be quartered in any house, without the consent of the Owner, nor in time of war, but in a manner to be prescribed by law.

3RD AMENDMENT

Limits on soldiers as mandatory roommates.

Ratified December 15, 1791

You can't be forced to house soldiers in your home during peacetime. You also can't be forced to host them during wartime, but Congress can pass a law that says otherwise.

BTW

King George used to make the colonists do this. They no longer wanted to do it.

United States

reply   favorite   hide   flag   Posted 45 minutes ago   print

No roommate during peace / TBD during war

Our guest room isn't available unless we're at war and Congress says it is.

*cats are OK
*dogs are OK
*Location: United States
*it's NOT ok to contact this poster with services or other commercial interests

Posting ID: 4829581952   Posted: 2020-04-14, 12:00AM EST

Amendment IV

The right of the people to be secure in their persons, houses, papers, and effects, against unreasonable searches and seizures, shall not be violated, and no Warrants shall issue, but upon probable cause, supported by Oath or affirmation, and particularly describing the place to be searched, and the persons or things to be seized.

4TH AMENDMENT

Uncle Sam can't search or steal you—or your shit—without reason.

Ratified December 15, 1791

People can't have their bodies, homes, papers, and belongings searched and seized without a reason to suspect they may have committed a crime. Warrants for searches and seizures are only issued if there's probable cause (a reason to suspect criminal activity). In those cases, to obtain a warrant you need to provide evidence under oath or affirmation, and the warrant must describe the place to be searched and the people or objects to be seized.

IMO

This amendment has been used to justify things like "stop and frisk" (police searches of people based on "reasonable" hunches) or to prevent illegally obtained evidence from being used in court. Also, we're all obligated to undergo searches *without* "probable cause" whenever we go through airport security (by the TSA) or security at a courthouse. Teachers and administrators have also been allowed to circumvent the amendment when searching students for drugs at school. But aside from these, one thing is clear: Madison was thinking about *physical* searches and seizures. I can't imagine that he considered blood tests from an unconscious person or data privacy from an unaware Internet user. Again, my opinion, but this is clearly an example of science and technology evolving beyond Madison's 18th-century grasp. I think it might be time for an amendment, and not just a law, that protects our rights in the digital age. In other words, maybe spend some time with the terms and conditions before mailing around your DNA to find new cousins.

Amendment V

No person shall be held to answer for a capital, or otherwise infamous crime, unless on a presentment or indictment of a Grand Jury, except in cases arising in the land or naval forces, or in the Militia, when in actual service in time of War or public danger; nor shall any person be subject for the same offence to be twice put in jeopardy of life or limb; nor shall be compelled in any criminal case to be a witness against himself, nor be deprived of life, liberty, or property, without due process of law; nor shall private property be taken for public use, without just compensation.

5TH AMENDMENT

You get a fair legal process.

Ratified December 15, 1791

You can only be tried for a capital crime (where the death penalty is possible) or another serious crime after a presentment (a formal non-written accusation) or an indictment (a formal written accusation) by a grand jury (between 16 and 23 U.S. citizens, whereas a trial jury is between 6 and 12 U.S. citizens). But the exceptions are for cases involving the army, navy, or militia (when they're in service during wartime) or during a public threat. You also can't be tried for the same crime twice ("double jeopardy"), and you can't be forced to testify against yourself in a criminal case. You basically can't be deprived of your life, freedom, or belongings without "due process" of the law, and you can't have your property taken for public use without fair compensation.

IMO

"Miranda rights" (cops informing the arrested of their rights, so that their statements are admissible in court) and "pleading the 5th" (not incriminating yourself) come from the Supreme Court cases around this amendment. Many cases also hinge on "due process," or on the fairness of legal proceedings. But the last part, about the government confiscating your property for public use if it pays you "fairly"? That's shady as fuck. It's called "eminent domain," and its inclusion in an amendment about individual rights is odd. Historically it has applied to things like building aqueducts or establishing national parks. Some states have written protections against eminent domain into their own constitutions. I think we could really stand to use some lasting clarification on the limits of eminent domain, because it definitely seems concerning.

Amendment VI

In all criminal prosecutions, the accused shall enjoy the right to a speedy and public trial, by an impartial jury of the State and district wherein the crime shall have been committed, which district shall have been previously ascertained by law, and to be informed of the nature and cause of the accusation; to be confronted with the witnesses against him; to have compulsory process for obtaining witnesses in his favor, and to have the Assistance of Counsel for his defence.

6TH AMENDMENT

You get a fair *and* a quick legal process for criminal cases.

Ratified December 15, 1791

If yours is a criminal case (e.g., an offense against the public like murder, theft, or assault), your trial must be fast and public with an impartial jury composed of people from the state, and the district, where the crime occurred. You must also be informed of the "nature and cause" of the accusation against you, and you have the right to confront the witnesses testifying against you (like, facing them in court while they testify). You can also force witnesses to testify on your behalf, and you have the right to a defense lawyer.

BTW

Trials can take years because of delays. But as for "public" trials, they really are open to the public (e.g., spectators, the media) unless the case is a matter of national security or if there's a public safety concern. This amendment also allows the defense to "subpoena" witnesses, which forces them to provide in-person testimony or tangible evidence on behalf of the defendant. If the defendant can't afford a defense lawyer, the court will appoint one (and our tax dollars will pay for it). Lastly, this amendment is why you have to do jury duty. Although I have to say, it's pretty incredible that a group of random and (hopefully) impartial citizens determines the guilt of a person. It is a truly powerful citizen role.

Amendment VII

In Suits at common law, where the value in controversy shall exceed twenty dollars, the right of trial by jury shall be preserved, and no fact tried by a jury, shall be otherwise re-examined in any Court of the United States, than according to the rules of the common law.

7TH AMENDMENT

You get a fair legal process for civil cases, too.

Ratified December 15, 1791

You're entitled to a trial by jury in civil cases too (e.g., an offense against a private party—like workplace discrimination, breach of a contract, or property damage) for disputes over $20. Your civil case can't be re-tried in the same, or in any other, federal court.

FYI

"Common law," as mentioned in this amendment, was a type of law in England that was based on judicial precedents and customs rather than on laws passed by a legislature (and where the remedy was money). Look, this isn't a particularly riveting amendment, but the takeaway is that you're guaranteed the right to a jury trial in *federal* court. But the weirdest thing FOR SURE is the $20 part. Adjusted for inflation, that's more than $550 today. But Congress quickly started raising the minimum amount, and since 1996 it has been $75,000. A federal civil case for $20 has never actually been heard, but it's still possible. Because Congress specified that both parties must be from different states or countries for the $75,000 minimum to take effect, it doesn't mention both parties being U.S. citizens from the same non-state in the U.S. So, if you're a U.S. citizen living in Puerto Rico, the U.S. Virgin Islands, Guam, the Northern Mariana Islands, American Samoa, or Washington, D.C., try suing a fellow citizen and resident for $20 in federal court and see what happens. It'd be a waste of taxpayer money—far more than $20—but according to the Constitution, you have the explicit right to do this.

Amendment VIII

Excessive bail shall not be required, nor excessive fines imposed, nor cruel and unusual punishments inflicted.

8TH AMENDMENT

No overly harsh bails, fines, or punishments.

Ratified December 15, 1791

You can't be made to pay excessive amounts for bail or fines, or be forced to endure cruel and unusual punishment.

IMO

Let's start with bail. There are multiple types, but I think "cash bail"—the process of using money as collateral so you don't have to sit in jail until trial—is unconstitutional. If you're a danger to society or a flight risk, you should have to wait in jail, or under house arrest, or in some other consistent fashion. But nowhere in the Bill of Rights, including in this amendment, does it say that you only get a right if you're rich. As for the third-party industry that traffics in cash bail (bail bondsmen), the U.S. is an outlier. In the entire world, only the United States and the Philippines (oddly enough, a U.S. territory until 1946) have legal bail bond industries. U.S. bail bonds are a $2 billion industry, but it costs U.S. taxpayers $15 billion a year to keep people (almost 500,000) in jail who are awaiting trial and haven't been convicted of anything. So American taxpayers are paying $15 billion a year so that bail bondsmen can make $2 billion a year in a business that debatably ethical and seemingly unconstitutional. I personally think we should end cash bail, and the industry on top of it, based on this amendment alone.

Now for "cruel and unusual punishment." It's vague and open to interpretation, but it's often understood to apply to barbarity (gruesomeness) or overly harsh sentences that don't fit the crime. There's also debate over whether the death penalty counts as "cruel or unusual punishment." Emotions aside, here's what I've learned. The U.S. is one of just 20 countries in the world that executed prisoners in 2018. On that list, we're number 7 behind China, Iran, Saudi Arabia, Vietnam, Iraq, and Egypt. Also 88 percent of criminologists say the death penalty is not a deterrent for criminals, and that sometimes it costs millions more to put people to death (because of the legal fees for long trials) than it does to keep people in prison for life without parole. This isn't even factoring in the reality that, in the last 40 years, 11 percent of those executed were found to be innocent later. In short, the 8th Amendment highlights criminal practices that are debatably ethical, debatably constitutional, pretty ineffective, and also pretty expensive to us taxpayers. Maybe that's why there's significant ideological concurrence around criminal justice reform.

Amendment IX

The enumeration in the Constitution, of certain rights, shall not be construed to deny or disparage others retained by the people.

Amendment X

The powers not delegated to the United States by the Constitution, nor prohibited by it to the States, are reserved to the States respectively, or to the people.

9TH AMENDMENT

Not all of your rights are in here.

Ratified December 15, 1791

Just because we listed a few specific rights DOES NOT MEAN they are your *only* rights (i.e., we may have forgotten some).

FYI

Madison is acknowledging that he may have forgotten to include certain rights in the Bill of Rights. As such, he wanted to ensure that the rights he didn't include could still be protected by the Constitution. To be honest, it's a pretty genius move. Also, since 1791, the Supreme Court has decided that these "unenumerated" rights include things like traveling, voting, privacy, and personal health decisions.

10TH AMENDMENT

If it isn't in here, the states or the people will handle it.

Ratified December 15, 1791

Any powers that aren't explicitly listed in the Constitution as federal government powers, or any powers that the Constitution explicitly says that the states *don't* have, are left to the individual states and the people.

BTW

This establishes that the federal government has *limits*. Perhaps more than any, a self-imposed cap on power is the ultimate check and balance—and thus a fitting end to the Bill of Rights.

Amendment XI

The Judicial power of the United States shall not be construed to extend to any suit in law or equity, commenced or prosecuted against one of the United States by Citizens of another State, or by Citizens or Subjects of any Foreign State.

11TH AMENDMENT

There are caveats to suing states.

Ratified February 7, 1795

You can't sue a state in *federal* court if you're a citizen of another state, or a citizen/subject of another country.

BTW

This amendment still allows you to sue your *own* state in federal court. But since its ratification, the Supreme Court has ruled that states must consent to federal *and* state lawsuits (which isn't in the amendment's text). This idea of governments being immune to lawsuits is called "sovereign immunity" (a dull legal term) and dates back to when you couldn't sue the king of England without his consent (because he was a tyrant).

Amendment XII

The Electors shall meet in their respective states and vote by ballot for President and Vice-President, one of whom, at least, shall not be an inhabitant of the same state with themselves; they shall name in their ballots the person voted for as President, and in distinct ballots the person voted for as Vice-President, and they shall make distinct lists of all persons voted for as President, and of all persons voted for as Vice-President, and of the number of votes for each, which lists they shall sign and certify, and transmit sealed to the seat of the government of the United States, directed to the President of the Senate;—the President of the Senate shall, in the presence of the Senate and House of Representatives, open all the certificates and the votes shall then be counted;—The person having the greatest number of votes for President, shall be the President, if such number be a majority of the whole number of Electors appointed; and if no person have such majority, then from the persons having the highest numbers not exceeding three on the list of those voted for as President, the House of Representatives shall choose immediately, by ballot, the President. But in choosing the President, the votes shall be taken by states, the representation from each state having one vote; a quorum for this purpose shall consist of a member or members from two-thirds of the states, and a majority of all the states shall be necessary to a choice. And if the House of Representatives shall not choose a President whenever the right of choice shall devolve upon them, before the fourth day of March next following, then the Vice-President shall act as President, as in case of the death or other constitutional disability of the President.— The person having the greatest number of votes as Vice-President, shall be the Vice-President, if such number be a majority of the whole number of Electors appointed, and if no person have a majority, then from the two highest numbers on the list, the Senate shall choose the Vice-President; a quorum for the purpose shall consist of two-thirds of the whole number of Senators, and a majority of the whole number shall be necessary to a choice. But no person constitutionally ineligible to the office of President shall be eligible to that of Vice-President of the United States.

12TH AMENDMENT

Choosing presidents and vice presidents.

Ratified June 15, 1804

The electors (Electoral College members) must meet in their state and cast their votes for president and vice president. Each elector must cast at least 1 of these votes for someone not from their state. The electors must specify which person they want for which job, then tally up the votes and send them to the president of the Senate (aka the current vice president). The Senate president will open and count the votes in the presence of Congress. If someone gets a majority of electoral votes for president, they become the president; if no one gets a majority, the House picks the president from the top 3 vote-getters. But in the run-off, the representatives vote collectively as the state they're from and *not* as individual representatives. To hold this vote, at least 1 representative from ⅔ of states (34) must be present, and a majority of votes is needed to win. But if the House doesn't pick a new president by—

N/A

This amendment says March 4, but Section 3 of the 20th Amendment changed it to January 20.

—of the following year, the person who was just elected the vice president becomes the president. Also the person who gets a majority of electoral votes for vice president becomes VP; but if no one gets a majority, the Senate chooses the VP from the top 2 vote-getters. To hold that vote, at least ⅔ of senators (67) must be present and the winner needs a majority of votes. Finally, if you're ineligible to be president according to this Constitution (i.e., citizenship, age, length of residency), you're also ineligible to be vice president. To sum it up: A SIMPLE PROCESS MADE SIMPLER.

BTW

In the 1800 presidential election, Thomas Jefferson and Aaron Burr tied in electoral votes. As the Constitution says, the House must now pick the winner where each state gets 1 vote and a majority is needed. But the House couldn't reach a majority after *35 consecutive tries*. And since the runner-up became the vice president, without a runner-up there was no VP and thus no one in line for the presidency. And since the Senate president pro tempore and the speaker of the House were the 2nd and the 3rd in line, and those roles wouldn't be chosen by March 4, the *4th* in line—the secretary of state—would be the acting president if the House didn't get its shit together. Finally, on February 17, with 2 weeks to spare—on the *36th* vote—Maryland and Vermont flipped to Jefferson, making him president and making Burr his vice president. Needless to say, this amendment sought to prevent such a situation from happening again.

FYI

The following is NOT in the Constitution; but so you're aware, here's how *voters* pick the president and vice president today.

Primary elections: Candidates for president seek their party's nomination in the "primaries," where each state holds a popular election—a primary or a "caucus." A primary is a state-run election with privately cast votes (your typical election), while a caucus is a party-run election with openly cast votes (like people in a room, raising their hand, or maybe walking to one side of the room). Anyway, these primaries and caucuses are held within 4 months of each other. As the candidates win the popular elections in each state, they collect "delegates" who pledge to vote for them at their party's convention in the summer. Some states award delegates as "winner take all" (where the popular vote winner in the state gets all the delegates), and some award them based on how many votes each candidate gets (it depends on the state). When one candidate gets more than half the party's delegates, they secure the nomination, but it isn't official until the delegates attend the convention and formally cast their votes. The candidate who wins the majority of delegates' votes must formally accept this nomination (so many formalities) to become the nominee. By this point, the nominee from each party has also picked a vice presidential nominee to run in tandem. When the conventions are over, the general election campaign begins.

General election: This campaign lasts 2 to 3 months, until Election Day (the 1st Tuesday after the 1st Monday in November because of the harvest). In 48 states, the winner of the statewide popular vote receives *all* of its electors (winner takes all). But in Maine and Nebraska (Nebraska does its own thing and I like it), the winner of the statewide popular vote gets 2 electors (for its 2 senators), and the winner of the popular vote *in each state's U.S. House district* gets 1 elector (for each representative). This is a hybrid of the statewide method (used by the other 48 states) and something called the "district method" (this was James Madison's preferred method). In other words, presidential nominees can split electors in Maine and Nebraska, which has happened twice (in 2008 and 2016). In total, there are 538 electors (for 435 U.S. representatives, 100 U.S. senators, and 3 for D.C. thanks to the 23rd Amendment). According to the 12th Amendment, you need a majority of electoral votes to win, and since half of 538 is 269, then 270 electoral votes gives you the majority. See? WE LIKE TO MAKE IT EASY.

IMO

The Electoral College winner has been different from the winner of the national popular vote 5 times: 1824, 1876, 1888, 2000, and 2016. As such, there has been a recent movement among states to grant their electors to the winner of the national popular vote. It's called the National Popular Vote Interstate Compact and as of this writing, it has been adopted by 15 states and D.C. for a total of 196 electors. If the elector total reaches 270, the compact takes effect for the participating states, enough to give someone the presidency. But there's also a debate over whether this compact is constitutional, because Article I, Section 10 says that "no state shall, without the consent of Congress…enter into any agreement or compact with another state." One argument *for* the compact is that states aren't creating a new governmental system, so *technically* it isn't expanding power beyond each state.

But as for the Electoral College itself, there's an argument to be made for reform. As of this writing, Texas has 1 electoral vote for every 551,015 voting-age residents, while Wyoming has 1 electoral vote for every 147,611 voting-age residents. Your vote for president shouldn't matter 73 percent less in Texas than in Wyoming. Also, Texas and Florida have 37.7 million voting-age residents with 67 electoral votes, while the least-populated 17 states have 18.6 million voting-age residents with 68 electoral votes. That's more electoral votes with less than half of the voting-age population. So there's an imbalance. But we've made changes to federal election methods before; in 1913, the 17th Amendment took the power to elect U.S. senators away from state legislatures and gave it to the people. In 2021, why can't we do the same with the president? There are 536 individual federal elections and 535 are decided by the people directly. I think we should make it 536 by creating a direct popular vote for president.

But I also understand the concerns. First, that a tyrant could become president. But if the people have been entrusted to directly elect all members of the legislative branch, they can be entrusted to elect 1 member of the executive branch. As for the concern about campaigns neglecting certain voters, under the current system nominees prioritize swing states. Without the Electoral College, they'd prioritize the largest cities. But what's certain is that candidates (who have yet to secure their party's nomination) spend far more time in the early primary states. The states that always have early primaries—particularly Iowa and New Hampshire—have an outsized influence on the nomination. But why do they always go first? Because their legislatures passed laws saying so, and the parties just went along with it. I think it's absurd. Other states could (and should) ignore this, which would probably lead to a legal challenge from Iowa and New Hampshire. Or Congress could pass a law establishing a process of setting state primary and caucus orders. Personally, I think it'd be fun to randomize the order every 4 years with a Powerball-style process. Being an early primary state is like winning the lottery: It's a serious economic boost to the state. As of this writing, it's estimated that 2020 candidates will spend $98 million on the Iowa caucuses and $178 million on the New Hampshire primary. You know who else could use that money? Every other state. Maybe one year it's Kansas and Connecticut, or Maine and New Mexico, or West Virginia and the U.S. Virgin Islands (territories don't vote in the general but they do hold primaries, so why not go there in February). Point is, whatever happens with the Electoral College, "Powerball for Primaries" is a way to spread out campaigns' attention and wealth so that the same 2 states don't always get the same cash prize every 4 years.

AMERICA 2.0

After 61 years, the longest period without an amendment in U.S. history, America got a reboot. Coming out of the Civil War, Congress and the states added 3 amendments in 5 years to grant several constitutional rights to African Americans and former slaves. But the enforcement of these rights was hindered. In the 12-year period following the war—called "Reconstruction"—there was a shitstorm of reactionary white supremacist violence and terrorism (e.g., the Ku Klux Klan, the White League, the Red Shirts). Then in 1876, arguably the most controversial presidential election took place. Samuel Tilden beat Rutherford B. Hayes by 3 percent in the popular vote and by 19 electoral votes (184–165), but the electoral voting in 4 states was delayed (Florida, Louisiana, Oregon, South Carolina). When they came in—and all went to Hayes—he suddenly had a 185–184 victory. Tilden's supporters went berserk. There was a plot to kill Hayes at his inauguration and someone even shot at his house during dinner. Congress quickly appointed a committee to look into the results. With a month to go until inauguration, a backroom compromise was struck. In exchange for Hayes removing the last of the federal troops from the South (in Louisiana and South Carolina), who were down there to enforce the 3 Reconstruction amendments (which we're about to discuss) and some federal civil rights laws, Tilden's supporters would recognize the election results without violence. This removal of federal protection left African Americans, who had voted for Hayes despite widespread intimidation and violence, to directly contend with Southern states whose governments had been taken over by white supremacists. In short, the gains for African Americans during Reconstruction quickly unraveled. During Reconstruction, there were more than 1,500 African Americans in local, state, or federal office, including 8 black U.S. representatives in 1875. After the backroom deal (aka the "Great Betrayal"), it would be another 94 years until 8 African Americans served in Congress. The reason I give this context is because this was the climate behind a large number of progressive amendments being proposed in such a short period of time.

Amendment XIII

Section 1.

Neither slavery nor involuntary servitude, except as a punishment for crime whereof the party shall have been duly convicted, shall exist within the United States, or any place subject to their jurisdiction.

Section 2.

Congress shall have power to enforce this article by appropriate legislation.

13TH AMENDMENT
2 SECTIONS
No more slavery—with an exception.

Ratified December 6, 1865

    Section 1: Slavery Is Mostly Over. **You can't force someone to work against their will—permanently or temporarily—unless you're punishing them for a crime where they were fairly convicted.**

    Section 2: Congressional Enforcement. **If needed, <u>Congress can reinforce this amendment with legislation</u>.**

IMO

The amendment's language comes from the 1787 Northwest Ordinance that banned slavery but permitted forced prison labor. One argument *for* prison labor is that some prisoners learn skills that may help them secure employment upon release. Some inmates have also written about the fulfillment they've found in the work that they did while incarcerated. But also, prison work continues to be a *very* cheap source of labor for governmental and private use. And if you broaden the range of imprisonable offenses, and crack down on arrests, you can increase this labor source. This happened after the Civil War when Southern states required African Americans to provide an annual proof of employment; when they didn't, they could be prosecuted, incarcerated, and punished with forced plantation labor (these were part of the Black Codes, which were Southern state laws attempting to limit black people's rights after the war). Also during Reconstruction, private businesses could rent prisoners from states in what was called "convict leasing," and then force them to work without pay.

As of 2017, 3 states—Arkansas, Georgia, and Texas—do not pay prisoners for regular prison jobs (e.g., janitorial work, kitchen work) nor for jobs related to state-owned businesses. And about half of states currently offer hourly wages that, on the high end, are less than $1. The Department of Justice even markets affordable federal prison labor to private companies. If this seems conspiratorial, ask yourself why a country with 4.4 percent of the world's population has 22 percent of its known prisoner population. Is it because Americans are 5 times more criminal than other nationalities? I don't think so, and I do think we need serious prison labor reform. Also, guess who else suffers when private companies and the government hire super cheap labor: American workers.

My diatribe is over.

Amendment XIV

Section 1.

All persons born or naturalized in the United States, and subject to the jurisdiction thereof, are citizens of the United States and of the State wherein they reside. No State shall make or enforce any law which shall abridge the privileges or immunities of citizens of the United States; nor shall any State deprive any person of life, liberty, or property, without due process of law; nor deny to any person within its jurisdiction the equal protection of the laws.

Section 2.

Representatives shall be apportioned among the several States according to their respective numbers, counting the whole number of persons in each State, excluding Indians not taxed. But when the right to vote at any election for the choice of electors for President and Vice-President of the United States, Representatives in Congress, the Executive and Judicial officers of a State, or the members of the Legislature thereof, is denied to any of the male inhabitants of such State, being twenty-one years of age, and citizens of the United States, or in any way abridged, except for participation in rebellion, or other crime, the basis of representation therein shall be reduced in the proportion which the number of such male citizens shall bear to the whole number of male citizens twenty-one years of age in such State.

Section 3.

No person shall be a Senator or Representative in Congress, or elector of President and Vice-President, or hold any office, civil or military, under the United States, or under any State, who, having previously taken an oath, as a member of Congress, or as an officer of the United States, or as a member of any State legislature, or as an executive or judicial officer of any State, to support the Constitution of the United States, shall have engaged in insurrection or rebellion against the same, or given aid or comfort to the enemies thereof. But Congress may by a vote of two-thirds of each House, remove such disability.

Section 4.

The validity of the public debt of the United States, authorized by law, including debts incurred for payment of pensions and bounties for services in suppressing insurrection or rebellion, shall not be questioned. But neither the United States nor any State shall assume or pay any debt or obligation incurred in aid of insurrection or rebellion against the United States, or any claim for the loss or emancipation of any slave; but all such debts, obligations and claims shall be held illegal and void.

Section 5.

The Congress shall have the power to enforce, by appropriate legislation, the provisions of this article.

14TH AMENDMENT
5 SECTIONS
A lot in the wake of the Civil War.

Ratified July 9, 1868

BTW

Madison helped here, too. One of the 19 amendments he drafted (reportedly his favorite) would've extended protections under the 1st and 6th Amendments (freedom of speech, trial by jury) to the states, so that state governments couldn't deny these rights to their citizens. The amendment cleared the House but died in the Senate. Years later, much of it ended up in this amendment. Anyway, the 14th Amendment also sought to help restrict the Black Codes while building on the Civil Rights Act of 1866 (the country's first civil rights law).

> *Section 1: Birthright Citizenship and Due Process for States.* **If you're born in the United States, you're a U.S. citizen and also a citizen of your state. States can't infringe on your federal rights and protections, and they can't deprive you of your life, freedom, and property without due process of *state* law (in the 5th Amendment, it was federal law). All residents of a state are also entitled to equal protection under the law (both state *and* federal, according to a 1954 Supreme Court case).**

BTW

This made free slaves—and their kin—U.S. citizens. It also protected individuals from abusive state governments by extending many of the rights in the Bill of Rights to the state level (called "incorporation"), even the ones that aren't mentioned in the Constitution (i.e., via the 9th Amendment).

IMO

Since 1868, the Supreme Court has used "equal protection of the laws" to prevent discrimination based on race, birth country, country of ancestry, religion, and citizenship status (it considers these groups to be "suspect classes," or people whose cases deserve the highest level of scrutiny). But besides granting marriage rights to same-sex couples, the Supreme Court has actually not extended the same level of scrutiny to prevent discrimination based on sexual orientation, birth legitimacy (wedlock status), or sex (hence the Equal Rights Amendment). It has also extended even less protection to people based on their age, disability, wealth, political preference, political affiliation, criminal record, or gender identity. In other words, it's up to each state to explicitly protect these groups with state laws. It's really hard to believe there isn't the same level of federal protection for all, or even most, of these groups. I think their sum, which is the majority of the population, deserves an amendment explicitly granting "equal protection of the laws." We're two decades into the 21st century; it's past time to be specifically protecting everyone equally.

Section 2: A New Representation Basis and Penalties for Denying the Vote. **The number of U.S. representatives from each state is determined by counting the state population, excluding Native Americans not taxed. But when the right to vote (for president and vice president, U.S. representative, state executives, state-level judges, state representative, or state senator) is denied to any *male* U.S. citizen and state resident 21 or older, unless they've rebelled *or committed a crime*, the basis for that state's U.S. representatives is decreased by the number of 21-and-up guys it won't let vote.**

BTW

This section ended the 3/5 compromise from Article I, where African Americans each counted as 60 percent of a person when counting a state's population to determine its representatives. However, this section explicitly *kept* the part about non-taxed Native Americans counting as 0 percent of a person (at the time, 90 percent of Natives weren't taxed) in determining a state's number of representatives, which prolonged Native Americans' status as non-citizens (they weren't granted citizenship until 1924). Lastly, the 14th Amendment *did* permit African American men to vote through their U.S. citizenship—and punished states with decreased representation if they didn't let them—but it wasn't a strong enough deterrent. So Congress had to explicitly add another amendment to say that U.S. citizens couldn't be barred from voting because of their race.

IMO

Like the 13th Amendment's "punishment" loophole for forced labor, there's a loophole here, too, for voting: "or other crime." In many states, this has been used to deny felons the right to vote even *after* they've served their time (it's called "felony disenfranchisement"). As of this writing, 3 states still have lifetime bans for former felons—Iowa, Kentucky, and Virginia—and many more prohibit voting during probation or parole. I personally think if someone has paid their debt to society, and has rejoined that society as a tax-paying citizen, they should have a say in where their taxes go. Maine and Vermont actually allow people to vote while incarcerated (Maine does its own thing and I like it). But as of this writing, only 18 states and D.C. restore felons' voting rights upon release.

Section 3: Rejoining the Government You Fought Against. **You can't be a U.S. senator, U.S. representative, or elector of presidents and vice presidents or hold civil or military office under federal or state government if you've previously taken an oath to support the Constitution as a U.S. senator, U.S. representative, federal officer, state representative, state senator, or member of the executive or judicial branch in a state,** *and* **you've participated in an insurrection or rebellion against the U.S. or helped its enemies in some way.** <u>**But Congress can remove this ban with a ⅔ vote in each chamber.**</u>

FYI

Technically this applies to any insurrection or rebellion, but it was pretty specifically prompted by the Civil War. In short, you don't get to rejoin the government you just tried to overthrow unless Congress says it's okay.

Section 4: Sorry, but Not Sorry, for Your Economic Loss. **No one can question the validity of the debt being incurred by the U.S., as long as it's authorized by law, including any pension or bounty payments connected with suppressing an insurrection or a rebellion (i.e., the one that just happened). Neither the U.S. nor any state is on the hook for debts incurred by funding a rebellion against the U.S. or for any economic losses because of no longer owning slaves. If the U.S. or a state** *has* **assumed these debts, they're now "illegal and void."**

FYI

In short, the government isn't going to reimburse you for trying to overthrow it—or for you no longer having slaves.

Section 5: Congressional Enforcement. <u>**Congress can pass laws to enforce the many things in this large and varied amendment.**</u>

Amendment XV

Section 1.

The right of citizens of the United States to vote shall not be denied or abridged by the United States or by any State on account of race, color, or previous condition of servitude.

Section 2.

The Congress shall have the power to enforce this article by appropriate legislation.

15TH AMENDMENT
2 SECTIONS

U.S. citizens of all races can vote.

Ratified February 3, 1870

Section 1: Voting Rights for U.S. Citizens of All Races. U.S. citizens can't have their right to vote denied or diminished—by the U.S. government or by their state's government—because of their race, skin color, or whether or not they were previously a slave.

BTW

This amendment doesn't say anything about sex, which means that states could still use it to deny female U.S. citizens the right to vote. And they did. It wasn't until 20 years later, in 1890, that Wyoming became the first state to give female U.S. citizens the right to vote. Fourteen other states would follow its lead before voting rights for female citizens was added via the 19th Amendment.

Section 2: Congressional Enforcement. **Congress can pass laws to enforce this amendment.**

BTW

Congress *did* pass laws to enforce *all 3* of the amendments, but the Southern states resisted. For example, their state legislatures specifically passed voting laws around registration that were designed to disenfranchise black men. They used *another* loophole, "not be denied or abridged," to create hurdles to voting rather than to directly deny or diminish the right to vote. These laws included literacy tests and poll taxes as pre-requisites for voting, as well as whites-only primaries. In short, I haven't really added many jokes here because in learning about the sheer lengths that certain state legislatures went to in order to create new iterations of slavery and racial disenfranchisement, it has honestly just made me sad.

On that note, this concludes the post–Civil War trio of amendments.

Amendment XVI

The Congress shall have power to lay and collect taxes on incomes, from whatever source derived, without apportionment among the several States, and without regard to any census or enumeration.

16TH AMENDMENT

Income tax begins.

Ratified February 3, 1913

Congress can set and collect taxes on your income, regardless of its source. The taxes aren't affected by, and have nothing to do with, how many people live in your state.

BTW

It's truly wild that no one in the country paid income tax until 1913.

Article XVII

The Senate of the United States shall be composed of two Senators from each State, elected by the people thereof, for six years; and each Senator shall have one vote. The electors in each State shall have the qualifications requisite for electors of the most numerous branch of the State legislatures.

When vacancies happen in the representation of any State in the Senate, the executive authority of such State shall issue writs of election to fill such vacancies: Provided, That the legislature of any State may empower the executive thereof to make temporary appointments until the people fill the vacancies by election as the legislature may direct.

This amendment shall not be so construed as to affect the election or term of any Senator chosen before it becomes valid as part of the Constitution.

17TH AMENDMENT

Senators are now elected by the people, instead of by the state legislatures.

Ratified April 8, 1913

Senators still serve 6-year terms, and each senator still gets 1 vote in the Senate. As with U.S. House elections, if you can vote in your *state's* house elections, you can vote in your state's U.S. Senate elections. Finally, when vacancies happen in the Senate, the governor of the state with the vacancy calls for a special election to fill the seat. Also, a state's legislature can allow its governor to appoint a temporary senator to last until this special election. These special elections are overseen by the state legislature.

BTW

This took the power that state legislatures had in the federal government and gave it to the people. Since 1913, citizens have elected 100 percent of Congress. As of this writing, only 5 state legislatures *don't* allow their governor to appoint a temporary senator when a vacancy happens: North Dakota, Oklahoma, Oregon, Rhode Island, and Wisconsin.

N/A

The final sentence of this amendment is no longer relevant, but it clarified that the amendment didn't affect the election or term of any senator picked before the amendment was ratified (pre-1913).

Amendment XVIII

Section 1.

After one year from the ratification of this article the manufacture, sale, or transportation of intoxicating liquors within, the importation thereof into, or the exportation thereof from the United States and all territory subject to the jurisdiction thereof for beverage purposes is hereby prohibited.

Section 2.

The Congress and the several States shall have concurrent power to enforce this article by appropriate legislation.

Section 3.

This article shall be inoperative unless it shall have been ratified as an amendment to the Constitution by the legislatures of the several States, as provided in the Constitution, within seven years from the date of the submission hereof to the States by the Congress.

18TH AMENDMENT
3 SECTIONS
Dry America.
Ratified January 16, 1919

N/A

This amendment no longer exists, as it was repealed by the 21st Amendment 15 years later.

Section 1: No More Booze. **Starting a year from ratification (in 1920), you couldn't make, sell, or transport alcohol anywhere in the U.S. for the purpose of drinking. You also couldn't import alcohol from, or export it to, other countries for drinking purposes.**

BTW

You could drink wine for religious purposes and prescribe alcohol for medical purposes, and lots of doctors wrote prescriptions then (11 million annually). About 1,000 doctors were caught selling prescriptions to organized crime members, and only 12 were indicted and had to pay, like, $50. Clearly this amendment was a joke, but my favorite part is that during Prohibition, Walgreens expanded from 20 stores to 525, and historians think that it was because of "medicinal" alcohol prescriptions. I'm not saying that Walgreens exists today because their pharmacists knowingly filled massive amounts of illegal prescriptions for booze, but also that's *exactly* what I'm saying. Historians believe Walgreens grew its store locations by 2,625 percent over 10 years because it knowingly filled illegal alcohol prescriptions for bootleggers, organized crime members, and probably your great-grandparents.

Section 2: Congressional Enforcement. <u>Congress, and the individual states, can pass laws to help enforce this amendment.</u>

Section 3: Method and Expiration. **Once the state legislatures receive this amendment from Congress, they have 7 years to ratify it—where ¾ of the state legislatures must approve it—otherwise it expires.**

BTW

The amendment was ratified in 13 months.

Amendment XIX

The right of citizens of the United States to vote shall not be denied or abridged by the United States or by any State on account of sex.

Congress shall have power to enforce this article by appropriate legislation.

19TH AMENDMENT

U.S. citizens of all sexes can vote.

Ratified August 18, 1920

The United States and the individual states can't deny or diminish a U.S. citizen's voting rights based on their sex, and **Congress can pass laws to enforce this amendment.**

BTW

The women's voting rights movement had begun 72 years prior, and was active during the 14th and 15th Amendment ratifications. Women were pissed about being excluded from the 14th Amendment (which specified males) *and* from the 15th Amendment (which specified race). As a result, movement leaders like Elizabeth Cady Stanton and Susan B. Anthony actually opposed the latter 15th Amendment even while supporting the 13th Amendment (to abolish slavery) because the latter didn't include them. By this point, the movement had reached a groundswell, and in 1919 the amendment was proposed by Congress to the states and ratified the following year. It's wild that there are still tens of thousands of people alive today who were around when women didn't have the right to vote.

Amendment XX

Section 1.

The terms of the President and the Vice President shall
end at noon on the 20th day of January, and the terms
of Senators and Representatives at noon on the 3d day of
January, of the years in which such terms would have ended
if this article had not been ratified; and the terms of their
successors shall then begin.

Section 2.

The Congress shall assemble at least once in every year, and
such meeting shall begin at noon on the 3d day of January,
unless they shall by law appoint a different day.

Section 3.

If, at the time fixed for the beginning of the term of the
President, the President elect shall have died, the Vice
President elect shall become President. If a President
shall not have been chosen before the time fixed for the

beginning of his term, or if the President elect shall have failed to qualify, then the Vice President elect shall act as President until a President shall have qualified; and the Congress may by law provide for the case wherein neither a President elect nor a Vice President elect shall have qualified, declaring who shall then act as President, or the manner in which one who is to act shall be selected, and such person shall act accordingly until a President or Vice President shall have qualified.

Section 4.

The Congress may by law provide for the case of the death of any of the persons from whom the House of Representatives may choose a President whenever the right of choice shall have devolved upon them, and for the case of the death of any of the persons from whom the Senate may choose a Vice President whenever the right of choice shall have devolved upon them.

Section 5.

Sections 1 and 2 shall take effect on the 15th day of October following the ratification of this article.

Section 6.

This article shall be inoperative unless it shall have been ratified as an amendment to the Constitution by the legislatures of three-fourths of the several States within seven years from the date of its submission.

20TH AMENDMENT
6 SECTIONS
Federal terms and presidents-elect.

Ratified January 23, 1933

Section 1: Term Ends and Beginnings. **The president's (and the vice president's) term ends on January 20 at 12 p.m., and the terms for U.S. representatives and senators end on January 3 at 12 p.m. These dates are also the start of the new terms for those offices.**

BTW

Again, those terms are 4 years for president and vice president, 2 years for U.S. representative, and 6 years for U.S. senator (also, the previous date for all of these people beginning and ending their terms was March 4).

Section 2: The Mandatory Meeting. **Congress must meet at least once a year—on January 3 at 12 p.m.—<u>unless Congress changes this to a different day by passing a law.</u>**

BTW

In 2019, the House's schedule had 130 workdays and the Senate's had 168 (129 overlapped). Compare that to an ordinary schedule, which had about 246 days. I know members of Congress travel to meet with constituents, but still, this feels light...

Section 3: Succession Scenarios for the President-Elect. **If the president-elect dies, the vice president–elect becomes president. If a president still isn't chosen or if the president-elect fails to qualify by 12 p.m. on January 20, the vice president–elect acts as president until a president *does* qualify. If neither the president *nor* the vice president qualifies, Congress can pass a law to choose an acting president—or a method of choosing an acting president—to serve until a president-elect or a vice president–elect does qualify.**

Another takeaway from the Constitution is that we've run into a very diverse array of unforeseen scenarios when picking presidents and vice presidents.

Section 4: Death During an Electoral Tie. When the House is choosing the president (when no one gets a majority of electoral votes) or when the Senate is choosing the vice president (for the same reason), if either choice dies, Congress can pass a law to decide what to do in this situation.

N/A

Section 5 is no longer relevant, since it said Sections 1 and 2 will take effect on October 15 following the amendment's ratification (which was 1933).

N/A

Section 6 is also no longer relevant because it said the amendment would take effect once ¾ of state legislatures ratified it, within 7 years of receiving it from Congress, or it would expire (it only took 11 months).

Amendment XXI

Section 1.

The eighteenth article of amendment to the Constitution of the United States is hereby repealed.

Section 2.

The transportation or importation into any State, Territory, or possession of the United States for delivery or use therein of intoxicating liquors, in violation of the laws thereof, is hereby prohibited.

Section 3.

This article shall be inoperative unless it shall have been ratified as an amendment to the Constitution by conventions in the several States, as provided in the Constitution, within seven years from the date of the submission hereof to the States by the Congress.

21ST AMENDMENT
3 SECTIONS

America is back off the wagon.

Ratified December 5, 1933

> *Section 1: Repeal.* The U.S. is repealing the 18th Amendment.

BTW

We're 4 years into the Great Depression. Let us have this.

> *Section 2: Obey the Law.* You must follow laws around transporting or importing alcohol for drinkable purposes into a state, a territory, or any part of the U.S. regardless of whether you intend to sell it or drink it yourself.

N/A

Section 3 is irrelevant because it said the amendment would take effect once the *constitutional conventions* in ¾ of states ratified it within 7 years of receiving it from Congress (or it would expire). It only took 10 months (Congress loved these 7-year windows).

BTW

Article V says that Congress can decide whether it wants state legislatures in ¾ of states *or* constitutional conventions in ¾ of states to ratify an amendment. It chose the former way for the 18th, 20th, and 22nd Amendments, but it has only ever specified the latter way for the 21st Amendment.

Amendment XXII

Section 1.

No person shall be elected to the office of the President more than twice, and no person who has held the office of President, or acted as President, for more than two years of a term to which some other person was elected President shall be elected to the office of the President more than once. But this Article shall not apply to any person holding the office of President when this Article was proposed by the Congress, and shall not prevent any person who may be holding the office of President, or acting as President, during the term within which this Article becomes operative from holding the office of President or acting as President during the remainder of such term.

Section 2.

This article shall be inoperative unless it shall have been ratified as an amendment to the Constitution by the legislatures of three-fourths of the several States within seven years from the date of its submission to the States by the Congress.

22ND AMENDMENT
2 SECTIONS
Presidential term limits.

Ratified February 27, 1951

Section 1: 2 Terms Max. Presidents can't be elected to more than 2 terms. If a president splits their term with someone else, and serves more than 2 years of it, they can *only* be elected to 1 additional term. This applies to anyone holding the office of president or acting as president.

N/A

The next part of this section no longer applies, because it said that when the amendment was proposed (in 1947), it wouldn't apply to the current president (Harry Truman). And when it was ratified (in 1951), it also wouldn't apply to the current president (also Harry Truman). Because he was exempted, Truman *could* have run again, but he chose not to.

N/A

Section 2 is also irrelevant because (you guessed it) it said the amendment would take effect once ¾ of state legislatures voted to ratify it, within 7 years of receiving it from Congress, or it would expire. It was ratified within 4 years.

Amendment XXIII

Section 1.

The District constituting the seat of Government of the United States shall appoint in such manner as the Congress may direct:

A number of electors of President and Vice President equal to the whole number of Senators and Representatives in Congress to which the District would be entitled if it were a State, but in no event more than the least populous State; they shall be in addition to those appointed by the States, but they shall be considered, for the purposes of the election of President and Vice President, to be electors appointed by a State; and they shall meet in the District and perform such duties as provided by the twelfth article of amendment.

Section 2.

The Congress shall have power to enforce this article by appropriate legislation.

23RD AMENDMENT
2 SECTIONS
D.C. gets electors (aka electoral votes).

Ratified March 29, 1961

    Section 1: D.C. Gets Some *Voting Rights.* **The nation's capital gets electors for president and vice president. They must pick the electors by whichever method Congress says. The number of electors is the number D.C. would get if it** *were* **a state (currently 3, as if it had 2 senators and 1 representative), but this number can't ever be greater than the least-populated state's electors. D.C.'s electoral votes are additional (i.e., we're not removing electors from another state and giving them to D.C.), and they carry the same weight as other electoral votes. D.C.'s electors also meet in D.C. and follow the process laid out by the 12th Amendment.**

    Section 2: Congressional Enforcement. <u>Congress can pass laws to enforce this amendment.</u>

IMO

This isn't in the Constitution, but like each of the 5 permanently inhabited U.S. territories/commonwealths—as well as the largest Native American reservation (Cherokee Nation, although Congress has yet to seat their representative as of this writing)—D.C. *does* have 1 representative… who can't vote. They can vote on procedural matters and sit on (and vote in) committees, but they can't actually vote on floor legislation. In full disclosure, I was born in D.C., and I lived there and went to school there, and I think this is bullshit. D.C. residents pay *a lot* of federal taxes; according to the IRS, in Fiscal 2018 (October 1, 2017–September 30, 2018) residents paid $28.5 billion in federal tax, more than 21 states and more than Vermont, Wyoming, Alaska, Montana, and West Virginia combined. D.C. also has more residents than Wyoming or Vermont, but 0 senators and 1 non-voting representative.

Since the 1960s, there have been dozens of D.C. statehood bills proposed in Congress, and a proposed constitutional amendment (the one from earlier) to grant it voting rights, but it expired in 1985. Every year since 1993 there has been a D.C. statehood bill proposed in Congress, but none of them got a floor vote. In 2016, D.C. residents held a statehood referendum similar to Puerto Rico's where 86 percent voted for statehood with 65 percent turnout. One of the leading arguments *against* D.C. statehood is that it would give the state too much influence on the federal government. To that, I'd argue you could carve out every federal building (and its land) from the state, not unlike how other states already do with "forts, magazines, arsenals, dock-yards and other needful buildings" (from Article I, Section 8). In 1959, we added Alaska and Hawaii as states. In 2021, why can't we add D.C. and Puerto Rico? It would also allow D.C. to finally stop stamping "taxation without representation" on all of its license plates (it does that).

BTW

America is actually the only democracy (representative or otherwise) on *earth* where residents of the capital city don't have voting representation in the national legislature.

Amendment XXIV

Section 1.

The right of citizens of the United States to vote in any primary or other election for President or Vice President, for electors for President or Vice President, or for Senator or Representative in Congress, shall not be denied or abridged by the United States or any State by reason of failure to pay any poll tax or other tax.

Section 2.

The Congress shall have power to enforce this article by appropriate legislation.

24TH AMENDMENT
2 SECTIONS
Poll taxes are canceled.

Ratified January 23, 1964

Section 1: No More Poll Taxes. The United States and the individual states can't deny or diminish a U.S citizen's right to vote in a primary—or in any other election—for president and vice president, for presidential and vice presidential electors, or for U.S. representatives or U.S. senators, because of that citizen's failure to pay a poll tax (or any other tax).

Section 2: Congressional Enforcement. <u>Congress can pass laws to enforce this amendment</u>.

BTW

This amendment only specifies federal elections (president and vice president, senator, representative), and not state and local elections, although the following year the 1965 Voting Rights Act allowed the federal government to investigate state and local poll taxes for voting. In 1966, the Supreme Court also ruled that poll taxes in state and local elections were a violation of the 14th Amendment. However, the 24th Amendment didn't include literacy tests, and only *some* of them were banned by the 1965 Voting Rights Act. After 1965, if you reached a 5th grade education in an American school where the predominant language was Spanish, you could be forced to take a literacy test to vote. Some tests even involved proving that you could read, and understand, the U.S. Constitution (ahem). This feels like a good time to mention that we also have a version of the book in Spanish (perhaps you're reading it right now).

In 1970, Congress finally banned literacy tests outright (but again, for federal elections), and that ban—along with other additions to the Voting Rights Act—was signed by Nixon and later made permanent by Gerald Ford (1975). The Voting Rights Act was further amended/extended by Ronald Reagan (1982) and George H. W. Bush (1992). The most recent extension of the VRA was by George W. Bush (2006).

IMO

Some have argued that if you require a form of ID to vote, and that ID costs money, then that's an indirect poll tax. Some estimates have priced the cost of a non-free ID, along with the cost of traveling to obtain it, at between $75 and $175. And if legal fees are involved, it can reach $1,000. In 2018, Florida voters passed Amendment 4 (with almost ⅔ support) to reinstate 1.4 million former felons' voting rights with a state constitutional amendment, but the Florida legislature then voted to allow this restoration only if the person has paid their outstanding fines and court fees (as of this writing, the case is being appealed). I know it's my opinion, but this definitely feels like a hurdle and a way to "deny" and "abridge."

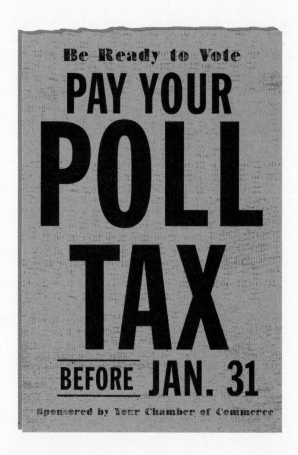

Be Ready to Vote
PAY YOUR POLL TAX BEFORE JAN. 31
Sponsored by Your Chamber of Commerce

Amendment XXV

Section 1.

In case of the removal of the President from office or of his death or resignation, the Vice President shall become President.

Section 2.

Whenever there is a vacancy in the office of the Vice President, the President shall nominate a Vice President who shall take office upon confirmation by a majority vote of both Houses of Congress.

Section 3.

Whenever the President transmits to the President pro tempore of the Senate and the Speaker of the House of Representatives his written declaration that he is unable to discharge the powers and duties of his office, and until he transmits to them a written declaration to the contrary, such powers and duties shall be discharged by the Vice President as Acting President.

Section 4.

Whenever the Vice President and a majority of either the principal officers of the executive departments or of such other body as Congress may by law provide, transmit to the President pro tempore of the Senate and the Speaker of the House of Representatives their written declaration that the President is unable to discharge the powers and duties of his office, the Vice President shall immediately assume the powers and duties of the office as Acting President.

Thereafter, when the President transmits to the President pro tempore of the Senate and the Speaker of the House of Representatives his written declaration that no inability exists, he shall resume the powers and duties of his office unless the Vice President and a majority of either the principal officers of the executive department or of such other body as Congress may by law provide, transmit within four days to the President pro tempore of the Senate and the Speaker of the House of Representatives their written declaration that the President is unable to discharge the powers and duties of his office. Thereupon Congress shall decide the issue, assembling within forty-eight hours for that purpose if not in session. If the Congress, within twenty-one days after receipt of the latter written declaration, or, if Congress is not in session, within twenty-one days after Congress is required to assemble, determines by two-thirds vote of both Houses that the President is unable to discharge the powers and duties of his office, the Vice President shall continue to discharge the same as Acting President; otherwise, the President shall resume the powers and duties of his office.

25TH AMENDMENT
4 SECTIONS

Filling presidential vacancies.

Ratified February 10, 1967

Section 1: *Presidential Vacancies*. If the president dies, resigns, or is removed from office, the vice president becomes the president.

BTW

As of this writing, this has happened 9 times (8 deaths and 1 resignation). The resignation was Nixon in 1974, upon which Gerald Ford, Nixon's vice president, became president.

Section 2: *Vice Presidential Vacancies*. If there is a vacancy for vice president (they die, quit, get removed, or ascend to the presidency), the president nominates a new vice president to be confirmed by a majority vote in the House and the Senate.

BTW

This has happened 18 times (9 ascensions, 7 deaths, and 2 resignations). The resignations were John Calhoun in 1833 and Spiro Agnew in 1973. After Agnew, Nixon nominated Gerald Ford to replace him, who was confirmed by a majority in the House and the Senate. And 8 months later, Nixon resigned, making Ford the president. A month after that, Ford gave Nixon "a full, free, and absolute pardon" for any crimes he "has committed or may have committed or taken part in" during his presidency. And people wonder why trust in our government has faltered.

Section 3: *Vice Presidents Acting as Presidents*. If the president writes the Senate president pro tempore and the speaker of the House to say they're unable to do the job of president, then until the president lets the Senate president pro tempore and the speaker of the House know they're able to *resume* being president, the vice president acts as president.

BTW

Section 4: If It All Goes to Hell. If the vice president and a majority of executive officers (i.e., the 15 Cabinet members)—or of another governmental body chosen by Congress—write the Senate president pro tempore and the speaker of the House to say that the president is unable to do the job, the vice president immediately becomes the acting president. But the president has the opportunity to respond by writing the Senate president pro tempore and the speaker of the House to say that actually, they *can* do the job, and those executive (or other) officers and the vice president are full of shit. After that, the president can resume being president, *unless* the vice president and a majority of executive (or other) officers respond to *that* letter—within 4 days—writing the Senate president pro tempore and the speaker of the House to say that *no, really, the president genuinely is unable to do the job.* At this point, Congress has 48 hours to assemble (if it isn't in session already) to figure this shit out. Congress has 21 days after receiving the 2nd letter from the vice president and a majority of executive (or other) officers, or if they *aren't* in session, 21 days after their sub-48-hour assembly, to vote on this. If they decide with a ⅔ vote of the House and the Senate that the president *isn't* able to do the job, the vice president continues to act as president. If the House and the Senate *don't* reach this conclusion by at least a ⅔ vote, the president goes back to being the president (followed by what I would only assume to be an extremely uncomfortable Monday morning Cabinet meeting).

WTF, America.

Amendment XXVI

Section 1.

The right of citizens of the United States, who are eighteen years of age or older, to vote shall not be denied or abridged by the United States or by any State on account of age.

Section 2.

The Congress shall have power to enforce this article by appropriate legislation.

26TH AMENDMENT
2 SECTIONS
U.S. citizens age 18 and over can vote.

Ratified July 1, 1971

> *Section 1: Voting Is 18+.* U.S. citizens age 18 and older can't have their right to vote denied or diminished by the United States, or by any individual state, because of their age.

BTW

As you may remember from the 14th Amendment, the previous voting age in the Constitution was 21 and older.

> *Section 2: Congressional Enforcement.* **Congress can pass laws to enforce this amendment.**

BTW

The push for this amendment began in the 1940s, but came to a head during the Vietnam War. The amendment was successful in large part because of protests by college students, and also the reality that individual states might have to maintain separate voter rolls for federal and state/local elections. The main argument *for* lowering the voting age was that if 18- to 20-year-olds could be drafted to fight in a war, they should also be able to decide who's shipping them off to fight in it. Hippies, man.

Amendment XXVII

No law, varying the compensation for the services of the Senators and Representatives, shall take effect, until an election of Representatives shall have intervened.

27TH AMENDMENT

Changing congressional salaries.

Ratified May 5, 1992

Any law changing the salaries of U.S. representatives and senators (in either direction, but really, "up") can't go into effect until *after* the next election of U.S. representatives and senators.

BTW

During the 1st Congress (1789–1791), each U.S. representative and senator earned $6 a day ($163 adjusted for inflation). If we applied that to Congress's 2019 schedule, representatives would earn $21,320 for 130 workdays and senators would earn $27,552 for 168 workdays. If they were paid for all 365 days, they'd have an annual salary of $59,860.

But if we took the $59,860 amount and multiplied it by the current number of voting representatives and senators (535), that's $32,025,100 in annual congressional salaries. But in 2019 we paid members of Congress $93,237,500, not including staff and expenses. Just pointing out that over time, adjusted for inflation, Congress has tripled its own salary.

BTW

As mentioned earlier, the 27th Amendment was one of 2 unratified amendments written by Madison that Congress sent to the states with the Bill of Rights. But here's the story of how it *was* ratified. Unlike modern amendments, the proposed amendments in the Bill of Rights didn't have expiration dates. So in 1982, 191 years after it failed, a sophomore political science student at the University of Texas–Austin named Gregory Watson noticed that some states *had* ratified it, but that it hadn't expired. So he wrote a paper about the failed amendment and got a C from his TA. He appealed the grade, but his professor upheld the C. Pissed off, Watson started writing letters to various state legislatures. They noticed and began ratifying the amendment. Ten years after his C, Alabama became the 38th state to ratify it, giving it the ¾ (38) needed to add it to the U.S. Constitution.

In 2016, Watson's paper was resubmitted for a grade change, with a request of an A+ for having caused an actual constitutional amendment. The University of Texas–Austin honored the change, but only gave the paper an A.

Those were the amendments, and that was the U.S. Constitution.

IN CONGRESS, JULY 4, 1776

The unanimous Declaration of the thirteen united States of America.

When in the Course of human events, it becomes necessary for one people to dissolve the political bands which have connected them with another, and to assume among the powers of the earth, the separate and equal station to which the Laws of Nature and of Nature's God entitle them, a decent respect to the opinions of mankind requires that they should declare the causes which impel them to the separation.

We hold these truths to be self-evident, that all men are created equal, that they are endowed by their Creator with certain inalienable Rights, that among these are Life, Liberty, and the pursuit of Happiness.— That to secure these rights, Governments are instituted among Men, deriving their just powers from the consent of the governed,— That whenever any Form of Government

becomes destructive of these ends, it is the Right of
the People to alter or to abolish it, and to institute new
Government, laying its foundation on such principles and
organizing its powers in such form, as to them shall seem
most likely to effect their Safety and Happiness. Prudence,
indeed, will dictate that Governments long established
should not be changed for light and transient causes; and
accordingly all experience hath shewn, that mankind are
more disposed to suffer, while evils are sufferable, than
to right themselves by abolishing the forms to which they
are accustomed. But when a long train of abuses and
usurpations, pursuing invariably the same Object evinces a
design to reduce them under absolute Despotism, it is their
right, it is their duty, to throw off such Government, and
to provide new Guards for their future security.—Such has
been the patient sufferance of these Colonies; and such
is now the necessity which constrains them to alter their
former Systems of Government. The history of the present
King of Great Britain is a history of repeated injuries and
usurpations, all having in direct object the establishment

of an absolute Tyranny over these States. To prove this, let Facts be submitted to a candid world.

He has refused his Assent to Laws, the most wholesome and necessary for the public good.

He has forbidden his Governors to pass Laws of immediate and pressing importance, unless suspended in their operation till his Assent should be obtained, and when so suspended, he has utterly neglected to attend to them.

He has refused to pass other Laws for the accommodation of large districts of people, unless those people would relinquish the right of Representation in the Legislature, a right inestimable to them and formidable to tyrants only.

He has called together legislative bodies at places unusual, uncomfortable, and distant from the depository of their public Records, for the sole purpose of fatiguing them into compliance with his measures.

He has dissolved Representative Houses repeatedly, for opposing with manly firmness his invasions on the rights of the people.

He has refused for a long time, after such dissolutions, to cause others to be elected; whereby the Legislative powers, incapable of Annihilation, have returned to the People at large for their exercise; the State remaining in the mean time exposed to all the dangers of invasion from without, and convulsions within.

He has endeavoured to prevent the population of these States; for that purpose obstructing the Laws for Naturalization of Foreigners; refusing to pass others to encourage their migrations hither, and raising the conditions of new Appropriations of Lands.

He has obstructed the Administration of Justice, by refusing his Assent to Laws for establishing Judiciary powers.

He has made Judges dependent on his Will alone, for the tenure of their offices, and the amount and payment of their salaries.

He has erected a multitude of New Offices, and sent hither swarms of Officers to harass our people, and eat out their substance.

He has kept among us, in times of peace, Standing Armies, without the consent of our legislatures.

He has affected to render the Military independent of and superior to the Civil power.

He has combined with others to subject us to a jurisdiction foreign to our constitution, and unacknowledged by our laws; giving his Assent to their Acts of pretended Legislation:

* For Quartering large bodies of armed troops among us:

* For protecting them by a mock Trial, from punishment for any Murders which they should commit on the Inhabitants of these States:

* For cutting off our Trade with all parts of the world:

* For imposing Taxes on us without our Consent:

* For depriving us in many cases, of the benefits of Trial by Jury:

- ✶ For transporting us beyond Seas to be tried for pretended offences:
- ✶ For abolishing the free System of English Laws in a neighbouring Province, establishing therein an Arbitrary government, and enlarging its Boundaries so as to render it at once an example and fit instrument for introducing the same absolute rule into these Colonies:
- ✶ For taking away our Charters, abolishing our most valuable Laws, and altering fundamentally the Forms of our Governments:
- ✶ For suspending our own Legislatures, and declaring themselves invested with power to legislate for us in all cases whatsoever.
- ✶ He has abdicated Government here, by declaring us out of his Protection and waging War against us.
- ✶ He has plundered our seas, ravaged our Coasts, burnt our towns, and destroyed the lives of our people.

* He is at this time transporting large Armies of foreign Mercenaries to complete the works of death, desolation and tyranny, already begun with circumstances of Cruelty and perfidy scarcely paralleled in the most barbarous ages, and totally unworthy the Head of a civilized nation.

* He has constrained our fellow Citizens taken Captive on the high Seas to bear Arms against their Country, to become the executioners of their friends and Brethren, or to fall themselves by their Hands.

* He has excited domestic insurrections amongst us, and has endeavoured to bring on the inhabitants of our frontiers, the merciless Indian Savages, whose known rule of warfare is an undistinguished destruction of all ages, sexes, and conditions.

In every stage of these Oppressions We have Petitioned for Redress in the most humble terms: Our repeated Petitions have been answered only by repeated injury.

A Prince, whose character is thus marked by every act which may define a Tyrant, is unfit to be the ruler of a free people.

Nor have We been wanting in attentions to our British brethren.

We have warned them from time to time of attempts by their legislature to extend an unwarrantable jurisdiction over us. We have reminded them of the circumstances of our emigration and settlement here.

We have appealed to their native justice and magnanimity, and we have conjured them by the ties of our common kindred, to disavow these usurpations, which would inevitably interrupt our connections and correspondence. They too have been deaf to the voice of justice and of consanguinity. We must, therefore, acquiesce in the necessity, which denounces our Separation, and hold them, as we hold the rest of mankind, Enemies in War, in Peace Friends.

We, therefore, the Representatives of the United States of America, in General Congress, Assembled, appealing to the Supreme Judge of the world for the rectitude of our intentions, do, in the Name, and by authority of the good People of these Colonies, solemnly publish and declare, That these United Colonies are, and of Right ought to be Free and Independent States; that they are Absolved from all Allegiance to the British Crown, and that all political connection between them and the State of Great Britain is and ought to be totally dissolved; and that as Free and Independent States, they have full Power to levy War, conclude Peace, contract Alliances, establish Commerce, and to do all other Acts and Things which Independent States may of right do. And for the support of this Declaration, with a firm reliance on the protection of divine Providence, we mutually pledge to each other our Lives, our Fortunes, and our sacred Honor.

BYE GEORGE, WE THINK WE'VE GOT IT

[George],

When the people don't feel it anymore, they should tell their political partners why that is. So here goes...

We think that all people are equal and have rights, and that those rights (e.g., life, liberty, pursuit of happiness) come from above. To protect them, people make governments, where they consent to being governed. If that government becomes destructive, the people can either reform it, or end it and start a new one. But we want you to know that this isn't impulsive; we've been feeling this way for some time. While lots of citizens stay in bad governments if they're tolerable, yours isn't. In fact, it's hell. So we're starting a new country. We've been patient, but you've been ruthless. For the record, we're talking about the following specific things:

1. You won't approve our laws.

2. You won't approve them even when they're urgent, either making us wait or ignoring us.

3. You won't approve our laws unless we give up representation, but we're not doing that. You seem threatened by this, which is how a tyrant would feel.

4. You keep an inconvenient schedule, and you make our lawmakers meet at weird times—in weird and distant places—to tire us into agreeing with you.

5. You eliminate our representation when we oppose you. You've done this several times, particularly when we disagree about our rights being violated.

6. You won't let us elect new representation after you eliminate our old representation. But you can't eliminate our legislative powers, since we're basically governing ourselves at this point. And you do realize that when you do this, you're leaving us vulnerable to invasions and uprisings...

7. You won't let our friends join us and you won't let us have more land.

8. You won't allow justice and won't approve our laws to establish a judiciary.

9. You buy off judges and make them dependent on you for their work and payment.

10. Your new employees are awful; they're messing with us and stealing our food.

11. Your old employees are awful; we aren't at war but your soldiers are just hanging out over here, which we definitely didn't agree to...

12. You're clearly trying to have them rule us.

13. You're trying to align with others to rule us.

Our lawmakers didn't agree to this, and we know that these new laws you're making aren't legal, like:

14. Forcing soldiers to live with us.

15. Not punishing your soldiers when they kill us; also, these "trials" in response to the murders are a joke.

16. Preventing us from trading with the rest of the world.

17. Taxing us without our consent.

18. Not allowing us to have trials by jury.

19. Kidnapping us and taking us back to England to stand trial for fake crimes.

20. Abolishing parts of our government, setting up new parts, and then trying to rule us through those.

21. Rescinding our charters, abolishing our laws, and changing our governments.

22. Suspending our legislatures and saying that only you can legislate for us.

23. Saying we're foreign and threatening war against us.

24. Plundering our seas, ravaging our coasts, burning our towns, and murdering our people.

25. Hiring people to come here and murder us barbarically.

26. Kidnapping us and forcing us to fight against our fellow

citizens. Or forcing us to choose between killing our own friends and family, or having them kill us.

27. Encouraging Native Americans rise up against us and murder us indiscriminately, including women and children.

We've complained about all of this before, but you keep doing it. A ruler who's a tyrant is not the ruler for us. We've warned your legislature about its continued illegal attempts to govern us. We've reminded them of the agreement we made in coming here. We've tried reasoning with them and reminding them that we come from the same place, with many commonalities. They don't care. So we have no choice but to become independent. These legislators and soldiers can be our enemies in war or our friends during peace.

Therefore we, the representatives of the United States of America in Congress—before God and with the consent of the citizens of these colonies—declare that we are, and have every right to be, free and independent states. We have no more connection to you, to Britain, to your crown, or to anything else of yours. And as free and independent states, we can declare war, make peace, set alliances, conduct business, and do pretty much anything else that free and independent states can do.

With God's blessing, we swear on our lives, our money, and our honor to support this declaration.

Or if you didn't have time to read all that:

Fuck off.

THE OMITTED PASSAGE OF THE DECLARATION OF INDEPENDENCE

He has waged cruel war against human nature itself, violating its most sacred rights of life and liberty in the persons of a distant people who never offended him, captivating & carrying them into slavery in another hemisphere or to incur miserable death in their transportation thither. This piratical warfare, the opprobrium of infidel powers, is the warfare of the Christian King of Great Britain. Determined to keep open a market where Men should be bought & sold, he has prostituted his negative for suppressing every legislative attempt to prohibit or restrain this execrable commerce. And that this assemblage of horrors might want no fact of distinguished die, he is now exciting those very people to rise in arms among us, and to purchase that liberty of which he has deprived them, by murdering the people on whom he has obtruded them: thus paying off former crimes committed against the Liberties of one people, with crimes which he urges them to commit against the lives of another.

OPPOSING THE SLAVE TRADE...SORT OF

You are beyond cruel for participating in the international slave trade, shipping off innocent people to be slaves on the other side of the world, where they may die on the voyage. You're obsessed with slavery and you block all attempts to end it. Now you're inciting slaves to rise up and kill us, as a way to buy their freedom from you. In effect, you're absolving yourself of your own crimes against humanity by promising their freedom in exchange for them murdering us (which is a crime against humanity).

BTW

Richard Henry Lee, a Virginia delegate at the Second Continental Congress in 1776, proposed independence. Thomas Jefferson subsequently wrote the first draft of the Declaration of Independence, and the other delegates (including John Adams and Benjamin Franklin) helped him revise it. Jefferson blamed the delegates for making him take this passage out, because *they* wanted to continue participating in the slave trade. But Jefferson would own 609 slaves. In short, the guy who wrote the Declaration of Independence with "all men are created equal" didn't exactly live those words. Jefferson is largely responsible for the document that asserted America's independence, which led to the Revolutionary War, the Articles of Confederation, and the current Constitution, but he also slept with a teenager that he owned and fathered 6 kids with her and enslaved 2 of the kids until they were 18.

In short? The people we idolize for doing amazing things are, simultaneously, capable of doing amazingly shitty things.

SOME THOUGHTS

No matter how you look at it, it's incredible that 55 European descendants—in less than 4 months—created a system of government lasting 231 years (and, as of this writing, counting). Although some countries have legal documents predating it, and Massachusetts and New Hampshire have older state constitutions (1780 and 1784), America has the oldest living constitution of any country. Imagine creating *anything* that lasts 231 years (starting now, that's through 2251) and *also* having it be the envy of the world (or wherever we're living). The Constitution's 3 branches and their 3 key relationships—to each other, to the state governments, and to the people—is a masterpiece. I truly believe that the Constitution is one of the greatest achievements in human history.

But while I'm fascinated by what's in the Constitution, the longer I've worked on this book the more I've become intrigued by what isn't. Such as...

Direct mentions of slavery before 1865. Contrary to popular belief, many of the Convention's delegates opposed slavery. A decade earlier, Thomas Jefferson trashed the slave trade in his first draft of the Declaration (although we know where he netted out on it). But when the Constitution was written, slavery was so profitable for tobacco, sugar, and cotton that the delegates just punted the issue 20 years down the road. And when the U.S. officially withdrew from the international slave trade at the first constitutionally permitted opportunity (1808), it would be 57 years before an amendment banned the domestic slave trade and the institution itself.

Native Americans, by and large. Besides being excluded from a state's population basis for its representation and taxation (on 2 separate mentions) and establishing that Congress can regulate commerce between the federal government and the tribes, there are no other mentions of Native Americans (although the Declaration of Independence does call them "merciless Indian savages"). This omission is largely because the tribes were sovereign and left to local control. But within the last century, a series of laws and Supreme Court cases have granted citizenship (1924) and voting rights (1948) to Native Americans, although it wasn't until Utah granted them voting rights (1962) that Natives could vote in every state. The 1965 Voting Rights Act also preserved and protected their suffrage. But as of this writing, Natives in some states are facing hurdles like state voter-ID laws that require physical addresses, which many Natives don't possess. As for taxation, Natives are exempt from federal and state tax paid on income earned on a reservation. There's also no state sales tax on transactions that occur on a reservation, and there are also no local property taxes. It's a unique dynamic where Native Americans are allowed to vote in elections for federal, state, and local government (which don't always apply to them), while not having *tribal* voting representation in Congress, and also being exempt from certain taxes. Continuing in the tradition of the United States' relationship with the tribes, the current state of affairs is a big fucking mess.

Voter registration and the elections process. The Constitution mentions elections and voting on several occasions, but there isn't anything about needing to register to vote. Since 1951, North Dakota hasn't required it. There's also nothing about state primary orders, nomination processes, debates, campaign contributions, and campaign lengths, because the Constitution says that state legislatures are responsible for deciding the "times, places and manner" of holding elections (although Congress can override these laws).

Lobbying. This is the practice of meeting with legislators or executive officers in person to influence their decisions around lawmaking and enforcement. Citizens can do this out of their own concern—and should—but corporations often send professionals bearing gifts like fundraising events and post-retirement board seats in exchange for certain action. The goal of corporate lobbying is to enact governmental policies that grow a corporation's bottom line. But while corporate lobbying isn't in the Constitution (as you now know), the Constitution *explicitly* bans "presents" and "emoluments" (gifts and payments) from foreign leaders and countries *without Congress's permission* (a potential loophole). The Constitution also says that presidents can't accept any emoluments beyond their salary from the federal government or any state's government, and that besides treason, bribery is the *only* crime specifically listed in the Constitution as grounds for impeachment and removal. The point is, the delegates were *extremely* concerned about bribery. Two hundred and thirty-three years later, it was for good reason.

Non-citizens' rights. Beyond restrictions on holding federal office, suing in federal court, or voting in federal elections, there's nothing in the Constitution that says its rights and protections are just for U.S. citizens. Historically, at least 40 states have allowed non-citizens to vote at some point for federal, state, and local elections. By 1926, every state had barred non-citizens from voting in federal or state elections. In 1996, a federal law explicitly prohibited non-citizens from voting in federal elections. As of this writing, there are still 11 states that allow non-citizens to vote in local elections.

The filibuster. The Senate tactic of open-endedly debating an issue, to avoid voting on that issue, is nowhere in the Constitution.

Executive orders. These are issued by the president to the executive branch, demanding that specific actions be taken with regard to law enforcement. They aren't in the Constitution, but they're considered constitutional as long as the law they're enforcing already exists. But in recent decades, executive orders have been used to almost *circumvent* Congress's lawmaking ability to legislate from the executive branch. Although unlike laws, executive orders can be reversed by the next president.

U.S. Department of Justice, Senate majority leader, White House chief of staff, etc. Some of the most powerful departments and jobs are absent from the Constitution. The DOJ was established in 1870, the Senate majority leader in 1920, and the White House chief of staff, in its current form, in 1953.

Political parties. They didn't exist when the Constitution was written, so I've left them out of this book. Our understanding of government is too often forced through their lens. Also, our first president never belonged to one.

But going back to what the Constitution *does* include, here's my biggest takeaway. I've been shocked to learn just how heavily our government was designed to rest on legislatures. Across all levels—federal, state, and local—the legislative branch is the engine that powers our government. Just look at Article I, and the insanely long list of congressional powers. Look at the references to state legislatures throughout the Constitution and how they're designed to be the engines of state governments. Our governing process is crystal clear on paper: legislators create laws, executives implement them, and judges settle their disputes. Which means that without legislatures, the executive and judicial branches would have nothing to do.

This makes perfect sense, because legislatures are the most representative branch of government *by far*. At the federal level we elect 0 members of the judicial branch and 1 member of the executive branch, but we elect *all 535 members* of the legislative branch. It makes further sense that the power rests in the most representative branch because our government was created in response to a monarchy. Whereas a monarchy has one individual ascendant by bloodline who rules through absolute government, a representative democracy has multiple individuals ascendant by election who serve through limited government. In a monarchy, the government holds its power over the people. In a respresentative democracy the government *borrows* its power from the people. With monarchies, if the people don't like how the power is being used, then tough shit—hopefully the ruler dies soon and their kid is less of a dick. But in representative democracies, if the people don't like how the power is being used, they can rescind it and give it to other people via democratic elections.

In his 1789 speech to Congress, James Madison called the legislative branch "the most powerful, and most likely to be abused, because it is under the least control." And in Federalist 10, Madison wrote the following:

> Men of factious tempers, of local prejudices, or of sinister designs, may, by intrigue, by corruption, or by other means, first obtain the suffrages, and then betray the interests, of the people.

If that quote rings true, then such a betrayal would foster distrust. Back in 1964, 77 percent of people said they trusted the federal government. In 1972, that number fell to 53 percent. It hasn't cracked 50 percent since. In 2019, as of this writing, the amount of people who say they trust the federal government is 17 percent. It is also 17 percent for Congress, which makes sense because 99.8 percent of our federal elections are for that branch.

I really believe this is an existential crisis for our country. People are fucking sick of congressional activity being corrupted by corporate lobbying, stagnated by hyper-partisanship, and rendered nearly impossible by the ridiculous amount of time required to fundraise. When 70 percent of the job is asking rich people for donations in order to keep the job, there's a larger problem at hand.

So what can you do? This book has focused on our problems and harsh realities. But this is the part about solutions. And while it may sound overly simple, in my honest opinion, the best way to start is by learning the answers to these 4 questions:

1. Who are my 2 U.S. senators?
2. Who is my 1 U.S. representative?
3. Who is my 1 state senator?
4. Who is my 1 state representative?
    a. Or if I live in Nebraska, who is my 1 state legislator (or "senator" as they're called)?

Putting aside local governments (since they aren't mentioned), according to the Constitution these 5 people are your single most important elected officials.

So here is my suggestion to you. Grab a bottle of wine, or a 6-pack, or light up a joint, or pour some herbal tea (this is an incomplete list) and cozy up in front of your computer, your phone, your tablet, or whatever, and see who your federal and state legislators are. You can do this by visiting bit.ly/findmyusrepresentative for your U.S. representative, bit.ly/findmyussenators for your U.S. senators, and usually by going to your secretary of state's or lieutenant governor's website (or just try Google). Visit their websites and read their positions. Google their names along with the issues you care about to see how they've voted (also, for Congress, GovTrack is a great resource). Maybe watch some videos of them giving speeches. In short, see if their views match yours.

Because while the president is obviously important—as are elected positions in the executive and judicial branches of states—the Constitution says that legislatures run the show. So instead of obsessively focusing on the presidency and the presidential election every 4 years, take that attention and shift it to your members of Congress and your state legislators. Because while the president and your governor are definitely needed to enforce the laws, and must "faithfuly execute" them, thanks to veto overrides they *aren't actually needed to make them.* And for further proof that legislative power trumps executive power, when it comes to amending the U.S. Constitution, the president is *nowhere to be found in the process.* It's like the president works for Congress, because Congress is the proxy for us.

But legislatures only work if they're held to account. And at times, this seems futile. It's like each of us is a drop in a bucket of corporate lobbying, hyper-partisanship, and gerrymandering (I have a whole journal on that). Or maybe some of us abstain from participating because the system wasn't designed to include us. These are all valid complaints. But the point of this book is not to berate you to vote, because so many people do that when elections near. The point is to share with you how government works, and by doing so to provide an understanding of what your vote affects, according to the Constitution. Because I think that if everyone knew all the things actually connected to their vote, rather than just hearing from people that it's "important" all the time, it might forever increase our appreciation and exercise of it.

But while voting is the most powerful thing you can do to influence our government, it isn't the only thing. Here are 3 ways you can interface with your representatives at the federal and state levels, to make sure they're representative of you.

Take a video of you talking to camera—addressing one of your representatives—and post it on social media, and tag them. Pick one of your 2 U.S. senators, your 1 U.S. representative, or your 1 to 2 state legislators—or do one for each—and speak about something specific you want them to do. Maybe you're encouraging them to vote a certain way on a bill, or asking them to introduce a bill to address a pressing need. Share a personal story about why this matters to you (don't use form scripts, people can tell if you're reading somebody else's words). What's great about tweets is that they're visible and searchable, so you're essentially putting your representatives on blast. Compared to writing a letter or an email, which they can throw out or delete (aka ignore), tweets aren't the same. This is highly public one-to-one communication. Facebook and Instagram are also great for this, but as of this writing elected officials tend to gravitate to Twitter.

Call your representatives. This isn't as public as social media, but it's harder to ignore ringing phones. Again, when you get someone on the phone, don't read from a form script—speak from the heart (think of Owen Wilson's toast advice from *Wedding Crashers*), use personal anecdotes, be authentic. And don't be a crazy person calling 10 times a day to scream. If the situation calls for anger, use it, but if you do that too often you won't be taken seriously.

Politely ask your representatives—by phone or email (it works here)—for an in-person meeting. See if you can meet with your federal representatives in D.C. or in their offices in your state, or in your House district. For your state representatives, see if you can meet with them in the state capitol, or in their office in your state house/senate district. Talk to them in person about what's important to you that they can do specifically. Be honest and forthright. Again, maybe it's getting them to vote a certain way on an existing bill, or to introduce a new bill. This is the type of citizen lobbying that's *supposed* to happen. Or maybe show up at one of their town halls (provided your representatives hold them; if they don't, be suspicious), and try to get face time there.

There are other things you can do to rally support from fellow voters or to volunteer around elections, like signing up as a poll watcher or attending a board of elections meeting. But the point is, many of these things are doable year-round, are impactful, and only require a small amount of your time.

In the 1876 presidential election (the very controversial one), the turnout was 82 percent of eligible voters. In 2016, it was 55 percent. As of this writing, America hasn't cracked 60 percent in over half a century. Judging by our current trust in government, it's clear that our country is lost. But when you lose your way, it helps to retrace your steps. And if you read the Constitution—our government's first steps—and trace its 3 branches, you'll notice that they all grow from a common source. It isn't party affiliations, campaign contributions, or corporate board seats after retirement.

ACKNOWLEDGMENTS

I'm not sure who reads this section, but these are the people who made this book possible.

Lisa Tenaglia, Becky Koh, Katie Benezra, Frances Soo Ping Chow, Hannah Jones, Melanie Gold, Lillian Sun, Betsy Hulsebosch, and Kara Thornton at Hachette Book Group and Black Dog & Leventhal. Thank you for believing in this, making it happen, and for being patient with my redundant questions.

Albert Lee, Byrd Leavell, and Dean Fluker at United Talent Agency. What began as a catch-up with Jonathan Levy (thank you, Jon) was followed by a hallway run-in with Dean, me mentioning this idea, him walking me over to pitch Byrd and Albert, and then 10 months later having actual books on shelves. I'll never get over it. Extra thanks to Albert for guiding a first-time author through a "crashed" book schedule and for letting me know when it's okay to sleep.

Dean Bahat and Ben Rubinfeld at Ziffren Brittenham. Thank you for not rescinding our friendship after my chaotic emails and phone calls.

U.S. Representative Jamie Raskin, Julian Davis Mortenson at the University of Michigan Law School, and Justin Nelson formerly at the University of Texas Law School, your notes were incredible and I'm forever appreciative.

Jesse Benjamin and Chris VanArtsdalen, for their brilliant design consultations and concept pitches.

Chad W. Beckerman, for your many hours of work from afar.

Joey Clift (Cowlitz), for sharing the side of America that was always here but that we rarely get to see.

Sophie Ragir. You saw the earliest iteration of this and encouraged it. Thanks for holding down the fort. I will always be grateful for your hard work and hustle.

Jackie Johnson. You tolerated more delayed arrivals, postponed plans, and conversations about the Constitution than anyone should reasonably have to. I love you.

Chooch, for not giving a shit about the Constitution and for just wanting belly rubs.

Arien Smith, for letting our workout sessions also double as therapy sessions.

Cody Horn, for being an unbelievably supportive friend in my political endeavors from pretty much the moment I moved to Los Angeles.

Ellen Goldsmith-Vein and Jessica Yellin, for being wonderful sources of guidance throughout multiple parts of this process.

Alex Richanbach, for your encouragement during our Sunday self-care and tequila sessions.

Jordan Brown and Kunal Tandon, for constantly being such kind, supportive, and encouraging friends.

Nate Ament, because I couldn't connect the fourth.

Robyn Bitner, for correcting me on the ConLaw terms I didn't initially grasp.

Jon Sheehan, for being the real inspiration behind this book. People like you who treat government as a tool to better our lives (as did mom) is something our media doesn't report. This book is also dedicated to you.

And lastly, to my teachers.

At Georgetown Day School:

Clay Roberson, for teaching a group of 13-year-olds that governments don't always have our best interests at heart. I've kept all of my class handouts, assignments, tests, and outside sources.

Bruce Snyder, for making calculus exciting and for making me realize that it's possible to make other seemingly boring things exciting.

Dana Krein and Chris Thompson, for giving the most thoughtful notes on assignments at the intersection of politics, media, and culture. I've kept most of my writing assignments from your classes.

John Frazier, Paul Levy, Morgan Kennedy, and Hayes Davis for the best class I ever took.

At Emory University:

Catherine Nickerson, Michael Moon, and Allen Tullos for creating an American Studies program full of relevance and reflection.

Merle Black and Harvey Klehr, for making southern politics and political theory both addictive and applicable.

Dwight Andrews, for elevating music classes to a level of political study beyond what I imagined they could be.

At New York University:

Catherine Montgomery, Charlie Sanders, and Judy Tint for your devotion, class discussions, and encouragement.

In Life:

Kevin Conroy, for telling me 15 years ago to cancel my plan to switch over to the undergraduate business school and to keep studying whatever I wanted. It was the first step along this path.

Ari Voukydis, for turning improv classes into masterclasses on listening, reasoning, and self-improvement. I still quote you 12 years later, and you have no idea.

My incredible colleagues from my Funny Or Die years, who are too many to name, but who taught me a masterclass in comedy by example.

And in light of the 9th Amendment, to anyone whom I forgot to thank, please know I'm no less grateful to you than to those whom I remembered to thank.

BIBLIOGRAPHY

PRE-PREAMBLE

Only 39 percent of adults can name the three branches of government.
"Americans' Civics Knowledge Increases but Still Has a Long Way to Go." *Annenberg Public Policy Center*. September 12, 2019. https://www.annenbergpublicpolicycenter. org/americans-civics-knowledge-increases-2019-survey/

Population estimates for territories. The World Factbook. Central Intelligence Agency. July 2018. https://www.cia.gov/library/publications/resources/the-world-factbook/

American Samoans aren't U.S. citizens. "American Samoans Aren't Actually U.S. Citizens. Does That Violate the Constitution?" *Los Angeles Times*. April 6, 2018. https:// www.latimes.com/nation/la-na-american-samoan-citizenship-explainer-20180406-story. html

Native American tribes, reservations, and population estimates. Frequently Asked Questions. U.S. Department of the Interior. https://www.bia.gov/frequently-asked-questions and Minority Population Profiles. U.S. Department of Health and Human Services. https://minorityhealth.hhs.gov/omh/browse.aspx?lvl=3&lvlid=62

Civics vs. U.S. history requirements in schools. "Most States Require History, But Not Civics." *Education Week*. October 23, 2018. https://www.edweek.org/ew/section/ multimedia/data-most-states-require-history-but-not.html (States requiring a year of civics/government: CO, ID, MD, NV, NC, VA, WV, WY)

K-12 civic proficiency hasn't reached 30 percent in two decades. The Nation's Report Card: Civics 2010. The National Assessment for Educational Progress. https:// nces.ed.gov/nationsreportcard/pubs/main2010/2011466.aspx and https://www. nationsreportcard.gov/hgc_2014/#civics/achievement

George Washington quote: *A primary object...*Washington's Eighth Annual Address to Congress. The Washington Papers at UVA. December 7, 1796. http://gwpapers.virginia. edu/documents/washingtons-eighth-annual-address-to-congress/

Thomas Jefferson quote: *Every constitution...*Source: Thomas Jefferson to James Madison. The Jefferson Papers at Princeton. September 6, 1789. https://jeffersonpapers. princeton.edu/selected-documents/thomas-jefferson-james-madison

PREAMBLE

Half of the delegates owned slaves. Historical Context: The Constitution and Slavery. The Gilder Lehrman Institute of American History. https://www.gilderlehrman.org/history-now/teaching-resource/historical-context-constitution-and-slavery

Slave population numbers. "The 1790 Census." *National Geographic*. https://www. nationalgeographic.org/media/us-census-1790/

THE ARTICLES

James Wilson, Charles Pinckney, James Madison, and the 3/5 Compromise. "Three-Fifths Clause." *The Heritage Guide to the Constitution.* https://www.heritage.org/constitution/#!/articles/1/essays/6/three-fifths-clause and "James Madison's Lessons in Racism." *New York Times.* October 28, 2017. https://www.nytimes.com/2017/10/28/opinion/sunday/james-madison-racism.html

Presidential succession. Presidential Succession Act. United States Senate. https://www.senate.gov/artandhistory/history/minute/Presidential_Succession.htm

Presidential indictments. "Indicting a President Is Not Foreclosed: The Complex History." *Lawfare.* June 18, 2018. https://www.lawfareblog.com/indicting-president-not-foreclosed-complex-history

Mandating the use of districts. The Apportionment Act of 1842: "In All Cases, By District." United States House of Representatives. April 16, 2019. https://history.house.gov/Blog/2019/April/4-16-Apportionment-1/

Can't gerrymander based on race, TBD on political party. Redistricting and the Supreme Court: The Most Significant Cases. National Conference of State Legislatures. April 25, 2019. http://www.ncsl.org/research/redistricting/redistricting-and-the-supreme-court-the-most-significant-cases.aspx#Race and Opinion of the Court. *Rucho v. Common Cause, Lamone v. Benisek.* June 27, 2019. https://www.supremecourt.gov/opinions/18pdf/18-422_9ol1.pdf

Election Day and the harvest. "Election 101: Why Do We Vote on a Tuesday in November?" *History.* August 31, 2018. https://www.history.com/news/why-do-we-vote-on-a-tuesday-in-november

Limits on time off to vote, by state. "In New York, California, Texas, and 27 Other States You Can Take Time Off from Work to Vote." *Business Insider.* November 6, 2018. https://www.businessinsider.com/can-i-leave-work-early-to-vote-2016-11

Government permission for post roads. "A New Look at the Founders Through the Postal Clause." *Independence Institute.* February 21, 2017. https://i2i.org/a-new-look-at-the-founders-through-the-postal-clause/

War declarations. Official Declarations of War by Congress. United States Senate. https://www.senate.gov/pagelayout/history/h_multi_sections_and_teasers/WarDeclarationsbyCongress.htm

Letters of marque and reprisal. "Marque and Reprisal." *The Heritage Guide to the Constitution.* https://www.heritage.org/constitution/#!/articles/1/essays/50/marque-and-reprisal and "Is It Time to Bring Back Letters of Marque?" *The Federalist.* March 25, 2015. https://thefederalist.com/2015/03/25/is-it-time-to-bring-back-letters-of-marque/

The Militia Acts of 1792, 1862, and 1903. The Second Militia Act of 1792. Original Text (Reprinted). https://en.wikisource.org/wiki/United_States_Statutes_at_Large/Volume_1/2nd_Congress/1st_Session/Chapter_33 and The Militia Act of 1862. Library of Congress. https://www.loc.gov/law/help/statutes-at-large/37th-congress/session-2/c37s2ch201.pdf and The Militia Act of 1903. Library of Congress. https://www.loc.gov/law/help/statutes-at-large/57th-congress/session-2/c57s2ch196.pdf

Women in the National Guard. "Women's History Month: Trailblazers in National Guard History." National Guard. nationalguard.mil/Features/Special-Features/Womens-History-Month/ and "History of Women in the Army National Guard." *Citizen-Soldier Magazine*. March 13, 2018. https://citizen-soldiermagazine.com/history-women-army-national-guard/

Thomas Jefferson owned 609 slaves. Source: The African American History Museum. *Smithsonian*. https://qz.com/891065/inside-the-african-american-history-museum-on-the-last-day-of-obamas-presidency/

Only since 1880 has every state held a statewide popular vote for presidential electors. "How the Electoral College Became Winner-Take-All." *FairVote*. August 21, 2012. https://www.fairvote.org/how-the-electoral-college-became-winner-take-all

Faithless electors are permitted in 18 states. Faithless Elector State Laws. *FairVote*. https://www.fairvote.org/faithless_elector_state_laws. (States: AR, GA, ID, IL, IA, KS, KT, LA, MO, NH, NJ, NY, ND, PA, RI, SD, TX, WV)

There have been 167 faithless electors. "Faithless Electors." *FairVote*. https://www.fairvote.org/faithless_electors

The 1st Monday after the 2nd Wednesday in December since 1948. U.S. Code Title 3, Chapter 1, Section 7. Cornell Law School. https://www.law.cornell.edu/uscode/text/3/7

Amendment that would've allowed Arnold Schwarzenegger to be president. "The Arnold Amendment." CBS News. https://www.cbsnews.com/news/the-arnold-amendment/

Current line of succession. U.S. Code Title 3, Chapter 1, Section 19, Subsection (d)(1). *Cornell Law School*. https://www.law.cornell.edu/uscode/text/3/19

Current presidential salary. "Here's the Last Time the President of the United States Got a Raise." CNBC. February 19, 2018. https://www.cnbc.com/2018/02/16/how-much-the-president-on-the-united-states-gets-paid.html

Oath of Office and God. "Who Said That? A Quick History of the Presidential Oath." *Constitution Daily*. July 12, 2011. https://constitutioncenter.org/blog/who-said-that-a-quick-history-of-the-presidential-oath/

State of the Union precedents. "State of the Union Address." United States Senate. https://www.senate.gov/artandhistory/history/common/generic/News_State_of_the_Union.htm

Not impeaching members of Congress since 1799. "The Constitution Signer Who Was Impeached and Expelled." *Constitution Daily*. https://constitutioncenter.org/blog/the-constitution-signer-who-was-impeached-and-expelled and "The First Impeachment." United States Senate. https://www.senate.gov/artandhistory/history/minute/The-First-Impeachment.htm

Congress set the number of Supreme Court judges at 9 in 1869. "Why Does the Supreme Court Have Nine Justices?" National Constitution Center. July 6, 2018. https://constitutioncenter.org/blog/why-does-the-supreme-court-have-nine-justices

Supreme, circuit, and district court judgeships. Authorized Judgeships—from 1789 to Present. United States Courts. https://www.uscourts.gov/sites/default/files/allauth.pdf

Supreme Court term limits debate. "The Continuing Debate over the Supreme Court and Term Limits." National Constitution Center. July 6, 2015. https://constitutioncenter.

org/blog/the-continuing-debate-over-the-supreme-court-and-term-limits/

List of impeachments. Senate Impeachment Trials. United States Senate. https://www.
senate.gov/artandhistory/history/common/briefing/Senate_Impeachment_Role.
htm#impeachment_trials

Deciding which parts of the Constitution apply to U.S. territories. "Downes v.
Bidwell: Does the Constitution Follow the Flag?" *Constitutional Law Reporter*.
https://constitutionallawreporter.com/2016/05/24/historicaldownes-v-bidwell-does-
the-constitution-follow-the-flag-2/

Federal property ownership. Federal Land Ownership. Congressional Research Service.
March 3, 2017. https://fas.org/sgp/crs/misc/R42346.pdf

Puerto Rico statehood referendums: 1967, 1993, 1998. Elections in the Americas: A
Data Handbook. Vol. I. Pg. 552, 555.

Puerto Rico statehood referendums: 2012 and 2017. "Low Turnout in Puerto Rico
Status Referendum." *Nationalia*. December 6, 2017. https://www.nationalia.info/
new/10981/low-turnout-in-puerto-rico-status-referendum-97-of-votes-for-us-
statehood and *Puerto Rico's Political Status and the 2012 Plebiscite*. Congressional
Research Service. June 25, 2013. https://fas.org/sgp/crs/row/R42765.pdf

Puerto Rico statehood poll. "Estudio Opinión Pública." *El Nuevo Día*. Junio 2017.
https://drive.google.com/file/d/0B-6drZFhVsMeU09VcEctNlBzNTg/view via https://
pasquines.us/2018/10/04/fact-checking-governor-ricardo-rossellos-claims-on-
statehood-for-puerto-rico/

Puerto Rico federal taxation in 2018. SOI (Statistics of Income) Tax. Internal Revenue
Service. https://www.irs.gov/statistics/soi-tax-stats-gross-collections-by-type-of-tax-
and-state-irs-data-book-table-5

State population estimates. Annual Estimates of the Resident Population for the United
States, Regions, States, and Puerto Rico: April 1, 2010 to July 1, 2018. United States
Census Bureau. Retrieved December 21, 2017. https://simple.wikipedia.org/wiki/
List_of_U.S._states_by_population

Americans supporting Puerto Rico statehood. "Americans Continue to Support
Puerto Rico Statehood." Gallup. July 18, 2019. https://news.gallup.com/poll/260744/
americans-continue-support-puerto-rico-statehood.aspx

Amendments introduced and proposed. Measures Proposed to Amend the
Constitution. United States Senate. https://www.senate.gov/legislative/
MeasuresProposedToAmendTheConstitution.htm "Proposed Amendments Not
Ratified by the States." Justia. https://law.justia.com/constitution/us/proposed-
amendments.html

Details of the signers. Founding Fathers. National Constitution Center. https://
constitutioncenter.org/learn/educational-resources/founding-fathers

State land size. United States Summary: 2010, Population and Housing Unit Counts.
United States Census Bureau. https://en.wikipedia.org/wiki/List_of_U.S._states_
and_territories_by_area

THE AMENDMENTS

Great rights of mankind. Madison's Speech Proposing Amendments to the Constitution. Teaching American History. June 8, 1789. https://teachingamericanhistory.org/resources/bor/madison_17890608/

Prior service requirements. Army National Guard. Eligibility. https://nationalguard.com/eligibility

Non-prior service requirements. Army National Guard. Eligibility—Prior Service. https://nationalguard.com/eligibility/prior-service

Diversity jurisdiction omitting non-states. U.S. Code Title 28, Part IV, Chapter 85, Section 1332. Cornell Law School. https://www.law.cornell.edu/uscode/text/28/1332

Bail bonds are a $2 billion industry. "How the Bail Bond Industry Became a $2 Billion Business." *Global Citizen.* January 31, 2019. https://www.globalcitizen.org/en/content/bail-bond-industry-2-billion-poverty/

Bail bonds cost taxpayers $15 billion annually and almost 500,000 people in jail haven't been convicted of anything. "Our Bail System Costs the Country $15 Billion Per Year." *Pacific Standard.* December 20, 2018. https://psmag.com/economics/our-bail-system-costs-the-country-15-billion-per-year

The U.S. is #7 on the list of 20 countries that executed prisoners in 2018. *Death Sentences and Executions 2018.* Amnesty International. https://www.amnesty.org/download/Documents/ACT5098702019ENGLISH.PDF

88 percent of criminologists think that the death penalty isn't a deterrent, and it costs more to put people to death than to jail them for life without parole. Facts About the Death Penalty. Death Penalty Information Center. December 7, 2016. https://www.supremecourt.gov/opinions/URLs_Cited/OT2016/16-5247/16-5247-2.pdf

In the last 40 years, 11 percent of those executed were later found to be innocent. "The Eighth Amendment: A Contemporary Perspective." National Constitution Center. https://constitutioncenter.org/interactive-constitution/interpretation/amendment-viii/clauses/103#the-eighth-amendment-a-progressive-perspective

Voting age population estimates by state. Estimates of the Voting Age Population for 2017. Federal Register. February 20, 2018. https://www.federalregister.gov/documents/2018/02/20/2018-03372/estimates-of-the-voting-age-population-for-2017

Iowa and New Hampshire. "Why Iowa and New Hampshire Go First." National Constitution Center. January 29, 2016. https://constitutioncenter.org/blog/why-iowa-and-new-hampshire-go-first and "Presidential Primary Set to Smash Spending Records." *Cook Political Report.* April 9, 2019. https://cookpolitical.com/analysis/national/political-advertising/onair-democratic-presidential-primary-set-smash-spending

Numbers of African Americans serving in office during Reconstruction. National Museum of African American History and Culture. *Smithsonian.*

Northwest Ordinance being the source of penal labor. Northwest Ordinance. Bill of Rights Institute. July 13, 1787. https://billofrightsinstitute.org/founding-documents/primary-source-documents/northwest-ordinance/

Prison labor as fulfilling. "Think Prison Labor Is a Form of Slavery? Think Again." *Los Angeles Times.* October 20, 2017. https://www.latimes.com/opinion/op-ed/la-oe-bozelko-prison-labor-20171020-story.html

Black Codes requiring proof of employment or slavery as punishment. "Black Codes." History Channel. October 10, 2019. https://www.history.com/topics/black-history/black-codes

Convict leasing. "Does an Exception Clause in the 13th Amendment Still Permit Slavery?" History Channel. October 2, 2018. https://www.history.com/news/13th-amendment-slavery-loophole-jim-crow-prisons

Prison wages by state. "How Much Do Incarcerated People Earn in Each State?" Prison Policy Initiative. April 10, 2017. https://www.prisonpolicy.org/blog/2017/04/10/wages/

The federal government markets prison labor to private companies. "The Federal Government Markets Prison Labor to Businesses as the 'Best-Kept Secret.'" Vox. August 24, 2018. https://www.vox.com/2018/8/24/17768438/national-prison-strike-factory-labor

The U.S. has 4.4 percent of the world's population and 22 percent of its known prisoner population. "Webb Says U.S. Has 5 Percent of World's Population, 25 Percent of Its 'Known' Prisoners." Politifact. December 15, 2014. https://www.politifact.com/virginia/statements/2014/dec/15/jim-webb/webb-says-us-has-5-percent-worlds-population-25-pe/

Madison's precursor to the 14th Amendment. "On This Day: James Madison Introduces the Bill of Rights." National Constitution Center. June 8, 2019. https://constitutioncenter.org/blog/on-this-day-james-madison-introduces-the-bill-of-rights

Suspect class. Suspect Classification. Cornell Law School. https://www.law.cornell.edu/wex/suspect_classification

Felony disenfranchisement statistics. "State Felon Voting Laws." ProCon. December 18, 2019. https://felonvoting.procon.org/view.resource.php?resourceID=000286

States that let women vote before the 19th Amendment. Centuries of Citizenship: A Constitutional Timeline. National Constitution Center. https://constitutioncenter.org/timeline/html/cw08_12159.html

States that prohibit temporary Senate appointments by the governor. Filling Vacancies in the Office of United States Senator. National Conference of State Legislatures. December 2017. http://www.ncsl.org/research/elections-and-campaigns/vacancies-in-the-united-states-senate.aspx

Prohibition statistics and Walgreens history. "The Lucrative Business of Prescribing Booze During Prohibition." *Atlas Obscura.* November 15, 2017. https://www.atlasobscura.com/articles/doctors-booze-notes-prohibition

Women's suffrage leaders opposing the 15th Amendment. "Women's History Month: The Legacy of the Fight over the 15th Amendment." African American Intellectual History Society. March 2, 2015. https://www.aaihs.org/womens-history-month-the-legacy-of-the-fight-over-the-15th-amendment/

Tens of thousands of centenarians in the United States. "World's Centenarian Population Projected to Grow Eightfold by 2050." *Fact-Tank.* April 21, 2016. https://www.pewresearch.org/fact-tank/2016/04/21/worlds-centenarian-population-projected-to-grow-eightfold-by-2050/

2019 Congressional Calendar. Download Roll Call's 2019 Congressional Calendar. Roll Call. December 12, 2018. https://www.rollcall.com/news/politics/roll-calls-2019-congressional-calendar

District of Columbia federal taxation in 2018. SOI (Statistics of Income) Tax. Internal Revenue Service. https://www.irs.gov/statistics/soi-tax-stats-gross-collections-by-type-of-tax-and-state-irs-data-book-table-5

District of Columbia statehood referendum. "DC Voters Elect Gray to Council, Approve Statehood Measure." *First Read—DMV.* November 9, 2016. https://www.nbcwashington.com/news/local/DC-Election-Statehood-Council-Seats-400275901.html

Some literacy tests were legal for federal elections under the Voting Rights Act of 1965. 52 U.S. Code § 10303(e)(2). The Voting Rights Act of 1965. https://uscode.house.gov/view.xhtml?req=(title:52%20section:10303%20edition:prelim)

Costs of obtaining voter identification. "'Free' Voter IDs Are Costly, Harvard Law Report Finds." *Harvard Law Today.* June 26, 2014. http://today.law.harvard.edu/free-voter-ids-costly-harvard-law-report-finds/

Florida legislature voted to reinstate felons' voting rights contingent on their payments of fines and fees. "A Controversial Florida Law Stops Some Former Felons from Voting. A Judge Just Blocked Part of It." Vox. October 19, 2019. https://www.vox.com/policy-and-politics/2019/7/2/20677955/amendment-4-florida-felon-voting-rights-injunction-lawsuits-fines-fees

Vice presidential ascents and vacancies. Vice President of the United States (President of the Senate). United States Senate. https://www.senate.gov/artandhistory/history/common/briefing/Vice_President.htm#3

Ford's pardon of Nixon. "Richard Nixon's Resignation Letter and Gerald Ford's Pardon." National Archives Foundation. https://www.archivesfoundation.org/documents/richard-nixon-resignation-letter-gerald-ford-pardon/

Section 3 of the 25th Amendment only used regarding the president's colon. "The 25th Amendment Has Been Used 3 Times to Relieve Presidents Deemed Unfit to Govern—Each Case Involving Physical Health." *Business Insider.* October 12, 2017. https://www.businessinsider.com/25th-amendment-colon-trump-reagan-bush-unfit-president-2017-10

Congressional salaries. Salary Storm. United States Senate. https://www.senate.gov/artandhistory/history/minute/Salary_Storm.htm and Congressional Salaries and Allowances. Congressional Research Service. April 11, 2018. https://www.senate.gov/CRSpubs/9c14ec69-c4e4-4bd8-8953-f73daa1640e4.pdf

THE DECLARATION OF INDEPENDENCE

Jefferson: Slave relationship, subsequent children, freedom status. "Hemings Gains Recognition in Recent Years, and Her Room in Monticello Is Now Part of the Historic Home's Tour." *Atlanta Journal-Constitution.* February 7, 2019. https://www.ajc.com/news/national/sally-hemings-thomas-jefferson-his-property/oKIBF28ni64Yv4i6x2NHJM/ and Thomas Jefferson and Sally Hemings. *Monticello.*

https://www.monticello.org/thomas-jefferson/jefferson-slavery/thomas-jefferson-and-sally-hemings-a-brief-account/

SOME THOUGHTS

Native Americans: Citizenship, voting rights, taxes. "The State of Native American Voting Rights." Brennan Center for Justice. March 13, 2019. https://www.brennancenter.org/our-work/analysis-opinion/state-native-american-voting-rights and "New North Dakota Voter ID Restriction Threatens Native Americans' Ability to Vote." *ThinkProgress*. November 2, 2018. https://thinkprogress.org/exclusive-new-voter-id-restriction-in-north-dakota-threatens-hundreds-of-natives-ability-to-vote-49937a379793/ and Do American Indians and Alaska Natives Pay Taxes? Frequently Asked Questions. U.S. Department of the Interior, Bureau of Indian Affairs. https://www.bia.gov/frequently-asked-questions

Non-citizens voting. "Political Rights in the Age of Migration: Lessons from the United States." *Journal of International Migration and Integration*. April 25, 2014. https://link.springer.com/article/10.1007/s12134-014-0336-6 and "Voting Rights: Earned or Entitled?" *Harvard Political Review*. December 3, 2010. http://harvardpolitics.com/united-states/voting-rights-earned-or-entitled/ and "House GOP Passes Measure Blasting Allowing Non-Citizens to Vote in Local Elections." NBC News. September 26, 2018. https://www.nbcnews.com/politics/congress/house-gop-passes-measure-blasting-allowing-non-citizens-vote-local-n913591

Madison's remarks about the legislative branch. Madison's Speech Proposing Amendments to the Constitution. Teaching American History. June 8, 1789. https://teachingamericanhistory.org/resources/bor/madison_17890608/

Trust in government. "Public Trust in Government: 1958–2019." Pew Research Center. April 11, 2019. https://www.people-press.org/2019/04/11/public-trust-in-government-1958-2019/

Members of Congress spend 70 percent of their time fundraising. "Unbreaking America. Represent Us." February 27, 2019. https://www.youtube.com/watch?v=TfQij4aQq1k&vl=en

Turnout in presidential elections. Voter Turnout in Presidential Elections: 1828–2012. The American Presidency Project, UC Santa Barbara. 2012. https://www.presidency.ucsb.edu/statistics/data/voter-turnout-in-presidential-elections and Statistical Abstract of the United States: 1932–2010. U.S. Census Bureau. 2012. https://www.census.gov/prod/2011pubs/12statab/election.pdf and Federal Elections 2012. Federal Election Commission. July 2013. https://transition.fec.gov/pubrec/fe2012/federalelections2012.pdf and Federal Elections 2016. Federal Election Commission. December 2017. https://transition.fec.gov/pubrec/fe2016/federalelections2016.pdf

INDEX

immigration, 40, 42

IMO, defined, viii

impeachments

House of Representatives and, 11, 15

judgment in cases of, 17

of justices, 67

presidential, 20, 63, 64

Senate's role, 17, 19

Supreme Court chief justice and, 17, 19

trial by jury and, 69

vice president, 63

imposts, 33, 36, 44

inferior courts. *See* federal courts

inhabited territories, 2

insurrections, 132–133, 137

intellectual property, 34

international slave trade, 40, 42, 189, 190

Iowa, 136

Jackson, William, 88

Jarvis Island, 2

Jay, John, 93

Jefferson, Thomas, 5, 39, 42, 61–62, 124, 189

Johnson, Andrew, 20, 64

Johnston Atoll, 2

journals, 24, 25, 28–29, 30

judicial branch. *See* federal courts; U.S. Supreme
Court

judicial review, 62

jury trial. *See* trial by jury

Kentucky, 136

Kingman Reef, 2

land disputes, 79

Lee, Richard Henry, 189

legal process. *See* fair legal process

legislative branch. *See* Congress; House of
Representatives; Senate; U.S. representatives;
U.S. senators

letters of marque and reprisal, 38

literacy tests, 163

lobbying, 191–192

local governments, 2, 103, 191, 192. *See also*
states/state government

Madison, James

on counting U.S. population, 13

14th Amendment and, 134

Jefferson and, 5

on legislative branch, 194

national capital and, 39

as secretary of state, 62

on writing The Bill of Rights, 93–94

Maine, 136

Marbury, William, 62

marque and reprisal letters, 34, 38

Maryland, 11, 89

Mason, George, 89

Massachusetts, 11, 89, 143

McCain, John, 53

Midway Atoll, 2

Militia Act of 1792, 38

Militia Act of 1862, 38

Militia Act of 1903, 38

militias, 34–35, 38, 56, 100, 101–102, 108, 109.
See also National Guard and Reserves

Miranda rights, 109

monarchies, 193–194

Muhlenberg, Frederick Augustus, 97

N/A, defined, viii

national capital. *See* Washington, District of
Columbia

National Guard and Reserves, 38, 101–103

National Popular Vote Interstate Compact, 125

Native Americans

Congressional representation and, 160

excluded from state population, 10, 13, 131,
135–136, 190

federally recognized tribes, 2

voting rights of, 191

natural born citizen, 53

naturalization rule, 33, 131, 179. *See also*
birthright citizenship

Navassa Island, 2

Navy, 34, 56

Nebraska, 12

New Hampshire, 11, 89

New Jersey, 11, 89

New York, 11, 89